I believe in Jesus

Minerva G. Carcaño
Study Guide by Glory E. Dharmaraj

Women's Division • The General Board of Global Ministries
The United Methodist Church

ISBN 978-1933663-18-0
Library of Congress Control Number 2007937608

Printed in the United States of America

CONTENTS

1 Opening Our Hearts to the Gift of Faith in Jesus Christ

L ong before I was born, Christian faith touched the life of my family. It was a gift that would shape and sustain my life. As a child I heard the story at the feet of my maternal grandmother, Sofia. It had happened when she was a young woman living on a sharecropper farm with her new husband, my grandfather Rafael. One day a man came to the farm unexpectedly. Tired and dusty from having walked the distance from the nearby town, he said he had come to share the good news of Christ Jesus. He wasn't a preacher, just a simple disciple whose life had been transformed by Jesus of Nazareth. It was not the first time my grandmother had heard of Jesus, the Son of God, but she had never met a person like this man before her; one who so loved Jesus that it moved him to share the gift of faith with her, a stranger. My grandparents and their large, extended family welcomed this man into their lives.

Over a period of several weeks this man of faith kept walking the distance out to the sharecropper farm where my grandparents lived and toiled. Every week he would speak to them about Jesus, sharing yet one more incredible story of wisdom, of healing, of power, and of hope. Then, one day, after having witnessed to all of the families on the farm, this man asked my grandparents and the others whether they would be willing to gather together for a time of worship. If nothing else, they had grown to love this man who so obviously loved them, so they agreed to gather for worship. As they began to gather they realized that they had failed to consider where they would gather. It was quickly obvious to them that there was not a single home on the farm large enough to hold all of them. These were resourceful people though, and soon someone said, "Let's just gather under the branches of the mesquite trees." So under the branches of the mesquite trees they gathered to worship God through prayer, the reading of Holy Scripture, and the singing of songs of faith.

My grandmother's face would light up and her voice would become even sweeter as she shared the powerful memory of that day. "It was under the branches of the mesquite trees that I felt the presence of God as I had never felt it before," she would say. Her favorite part of the memory was the singing of the songs of faith; it was then that she heard the voice of Jesus. "As we sang those hymns I heard Jesus call me by name and I could do no other than surrender my life to him," was my grandmother's witness.

My grandmother's faith nurtured a family for whom Christ Jesus was central. Our week was framed by Sunday worship, each day began and ended with prayer, meals were consumed only after giving thanks to God, Scripture was read with great discipline, and life was lived in the confidence that we were not alone for Christ Jesus abided with us in the fullness of his grace and his power. I was fortunate to be born into this family of faith.

We lived in the great poverty that even today is so prevalent in that extreme southern region of Texas that juts out into the Gulf of Mexico, and that exists side by side with Mexico along the Rio Grande River. By the time I was born my family no longer share-cropped, but still labored hard picking cotton, hoeing tomato fields and transporting the area's bountiful crops all over the country. Living in a region of great economic disparity where the minority

2

of white persons owned most of the land, and the majority Hispanic population worked in the fields, racism and classism afflicted our lives like a wound that never heals. Even then, joy prevailed for we were disciples of Christ Jesus, and in his name and his strength we could do all things. I remember when I first truly believed this.

As a child I did what many Hispanic children have had to do to help their families survive. I worked in the fields whose fruit has clothed and fed others across the United States. My father came to the United States as a *bracero* (a laborer brought to this country through a labor agreement reached with the Mexican government during World War II). With many men off to war, the United States found itself without sufficient laborers to plant and pick the crops that sustained the American populace. Later he worked as a butcher and, finally, for a paper company that made boxes for the area's produce. My father ran the machine that coated the boxes in thick wax in order to protect the freshness of the produce. My father worked very hard, but received low wages, and with a growing family he could not earn enough to keep us all fed. So for a time my mother, two of my brothers, and I cleaned fields and picked cotton. One of my sisters stayed home with our grandmother to help her as she cared for my younger siblings.

My mother, brothers, and I worked in the fields from five o'clock in the morning until sunset. As a child not yet a teenager, I was very proud of the fact that on a good day I could pick 125 pounds of cotton. I aspired to be as good a cotton picker as my mother who could pick 300 pounds of cotton a day. My two younger brothers shared a cotton sack and were happy when they picked fifty pounds together throughout a day. For our very long days of work we were paid $2.25 for every 100 pounds of cotton we picked. It was backbreaking work. We always had scratched and cut arms and hands. Playtime was what little time we could steal in the cotton fields when we took a lunch break or when no one was looking.

Amazingly, there were things I enjoyed about the experience. I enjoyed being with my mother. I grew to enjoy the still beauty of dawn. I loved the sweet, hot coffee and the tortillas filled with refried pinto beans that we ate under the trees in the cotton fields. And, I have never slept better than I slept during those years of field labor. But, there were also those horrible days when I thought we would certainly be destroyed by the work, consumed by its demands. I recall such a day.

We were the only cotton pickers on what seemed to be the biggest cotton field in all of Texas! My mother was picking the cotton on the row to my left, and my brothers were picking the row to my right. The hot July sun was beating down on us relentlessly with all of its intensity. While I struggled with my row of cotton, my mother moved far ahead of me and my brothers picked and played behind me. My back ached, my hands were bleeding, and I felt despair at not being able to even see the end of the cotton row. But just at the point when I thought that I could go no further and would surely die in the middle of that field, I looked up and found myself face-to-face with my mother. She had finished picking her row and had picked my row all the way to where I was. As I looked into her determined eyes right before me, she said to me, "My precious daughter, never forget that we can 'do all things through him who strengthens [us]'" (Philippians 4:13). With that she finished picking my row of cotton and invited me to follow her in helping my brothers finish theirs, and I believed! I believed that we could conquer not only that cotton field, but also all of life's struggles.

In that moment it was as if my mother had given me a large glass of cold, refreshing water. I felt her cover me from the glaring sun, take me under her wings, and carry me to the end of the cotton row. It was, of course, Christ's sustaining mercy that she had shared with me. Because of her own faith, my mother could see beyond the long rows of cotton, beyond the blinding sun, beyond the brokenness of our bodies, beyond the despair of our poverty. She could see all the way to Jesus who she knew as the source of strength and life for her living and ours. And through her eyes, I too believed. I believed that Jesus cared about us and accompanied us with mercy and grace even in the cotton fields. It was a day when my faith in Jesus grew. Not long after that, however, my faith was shaken to the core.

A few days after celebrating my sixteenth birthday it was discovered that my beloved grandmother Sofia had an incurable disease. She had been ill for several months but the doctors had failed to determine the cause of her illness. Now they knew and informed us that it would be but a matter of days, perhaps weeks, until the illness would completely consume her. To say that we were all devastated is not enough. She was the pillar of faith in our family. How would we survive without her? Each one of us dealt with this word of death in our own way. My mother, my grandmother's only daughter, prepared to care for her mother, praying that God's miracle of healing would come. I, on the other hand, found it difficult to pray, and became so very aware of how much my faith was dependent on my grandmother's faith. I was old enough to know about death and dying, old enough to address my grandmother's imminent death through faith. I was old enough, but it did not make any difference.

One evening, to give my mother a much-needed night's sleep, I went and stayed with my grandmother at the hospital. My grandmother was dying of cancer, and at one point in the night she turned away from me in her bed. Her hospital gown fell open across her back and I could see mounds of trembling flesh where the cancer was growing and consuming her. As she turned away I could hear my grandmother praising God as she recited her favorite Psalms:

> The Lord is my shepherd, I shall not want....
> The Lord is my light and my salvation, whom
> shall I fear?…Surely I would have fainted were it not
> that I believe that I shall see the Lord in the land of
> the living.
>
> (From Psalms 23, 27)

Then it happened—I snapped, rebelled against God, and cursed God. The rebellion and the cursing were all in my mind and in my heart. I said nothing aloud, but my grandmother in her spirit sensed the state of my spirit, and she turned back towards me and said to me:

> Don't be angry with God. I have lived a good life.
> God has been gracious and merciful toward me and mine.
> In life's struggles Christ Jesus has sustained me.
> It is my precious Lord who has made my joy complete.
> And it is Jesus' face that I now long to see, his arms I long
>   to be in.
> I am ready. My life is at peace because of my Savior.

On the day we buried my grandmother I experienced the peace of which she spoke, a peace beyond my understanding but a peace that touched my life with the assurance that God was present, lovingly and powerfully breaking the bonds of death through Christ Jesus and healing our hurting hearts. It was then, through the care of my grandmother Sofia, that I believed, truly believed, that Jesus is the Christ. Walking through my rebellion of faith, I found Jesus waiting for me, grace-filled. In that moment, faith in

Christ Jesus became mine and not my grandmother's, as much as I will always thank God for her witness in my life that led me to Jesus. I am reminded of the apostle Paul's words to young Timothy when he affirms that the faith that had first lived in his grandmother and his mother now lived in him (II Timothy 1:5b). It was an inescapable moment in my life, and I found Jesus faithful. It is the experience of every generation of those who open their hearts to Christ Jesus.

The early Christians had to find Jesus for themselves. Those of Jewish descent had to determine whether Jesus was indeed the fulfillment of the prophetic promise of the Messiah. Could Jesus be the servant that the prophet Isaiah had spoken of, the Chosen One of God upon whom God's own spirit would rest bringing forth justice to the nations? Our families of faith inform our faith and nurture us in faith, but, as I learned in the death of my grandmother, belief in Jesus is a matter of personal encounter with the Holy.

Such was the experience of the early Jewish converts who, after Pentecost and upon hearing the witness of Peter about Jesus of Nazareth, "were cut to the heart and said to Peter and to the other apostles, 'Brothers, what should we do?'" (Acts 2:37). Peter invited them to repent of their sins, believe in Jesus Christ, and receive the Holy Spirit. Believing, they were baptized in the name of Jesus Christ and joined the fellowship of Christians, learning under the care of the apostles, breaking bread and praying together, and sharing all things in common (Acts 2:42-47).

Gentiles, no less than Jews, were touched by the Holy Spirit unto faith in Jesus Christ. The story of Cornelius, the first Gentile convert, is a witness to God's prevenient grace. Even before we are aware of God's presence in our lives and in our hearts, God's spirit is at work convincing us of our need of God. Cornelius feared God before knowing Christ Jesus. A centurion of the Italian Cohort, Cornelius was a well-respected man who one day had a vision of an angel of God coming close and calling him by name. The angel had a message for Cornelius from God. He was to invite Peter to his home for God had more to give him for his journey of faith. This was no simple request for Cornelius was a Gentile and Peter was a Jew. They were men of two different and estranged cultures, but Cornelius was obedient to the movement of God's spirit in his life and sent for Peter (Acts 10:1-8).

Peter's recorded struggle with his own beliefs about Gentiles comes to us as a clear witness to the universality of God's love through Jesus Christ. While Cornelius received a God-given vision that led him to invite Peter to his home, God's spirit was at work in Peter's heart through a trance that led him to the faith, understanding that what God has made clean must not be called profane (Acts 10:9-16). Peter and his Jewish community believed that Gentiles were profane for they had none of the outer signs of faith. It was true that the Gentiles did not practice the covenant act of male circumcision nor did they observe the table rituals of the Jewish faith. God, however, was doing a new thing through Jesus Christ.

Led by God to Cornelius and his faith, Peter came to believe that God shows no partiality. Rather, in every nation, all who fear God and do what is right are acceptable to God (Acts 10:34-35). It was in believing that God's gift of faith is for all the world that Peter was then able to give a witness of peace to Cornelius, a Gentile, and to all his household, as he proclaimed that Jesus Christ is Lord of all (Acts 10:36). The story of Peter and Cornelius in Acts is an incredible story of how faith in Jesus Christ transforms lives and breaks down barriers.

Gentile and Jew learned that faith in Jesus not only challenges assumptions about persons, cultures, social status, and even religious mores, but also transforms persons, making of those who believe a community of grace and power. The stories of Philip and the Ethiopian eunuch (Acts 8:26-39), and of Paul and Lydia (Acts 16:11-15), also continue to speak to us today of God's love for all persons, a love we come to know most fully through God's gift of Jesus Christ.

The acceptance of the Gentiles into the Jewish Christian community took much work. Ultimately it was the Spirit-led recognition that God was cleansing the hearts of Gentiles and Jews alike, and the memory of the words of the prophets that led the Jewish Christians to make room for the Gentile converts to form one large Christian community (Isaiah 54:1-5; Hosea 3:5; Amos 9:11; Micah 5:2). The prophet Isaiah had one day lifted up the powerful images of the suffering servant who would bring justice to the nations, and of the Jewish faithful, the people of the covenant, who would serve God as a light to the nations (Isaiah 42:1-11). Openness to the promise of God's redemption for all people through Jesus Christ and Israel's active role in that redemptive activity came slowly but surely to the early Jewish Christians. Even as they debated the very possibility that salvation in Christ Jesus was also intended for the Gentiles, men and women of Gentile identity were responding to the good news. Acts 15 shares the story of human debate and determination and divine grace and acceptance.

Some of the early Gentiles who became believers in Christ Jesus were touched by the good news long before Jewish Christians ever reached out to them. Trying to catch up with the work of the Holy Spirit already confirmed in Gentile hearts, some Jewish Christians came to them and proclaimed that their faith was not authentic and that, in fact, if they were not circumcised according to the custom of Moses, they could not be saved (Acts 15:1). This incident created such a controversy that a Council was called in Jerusalem to discuss the matter. Paul and Barnabas were among those elected to go and confer with the apostles and the elders in

Jerusalem. Further weighing in on the discussion at hand, the Holy Spirit worked through Paul and Barnabas extending grace and redemption to persons in the Gentile regions of Phoenicia and Samaria as they traveled through them on the way to Jerusalem. Paul and Barnabas joyfully took this witness to the Council at Jerusalem. Their joy was met with some resistance by those who belonged to the sect of the Pharisees and who continued to insist on circumcision and the keeping of the law of Moses (Acts 15:5). In the end divine grace and acceptance had the last word.

Addressing the Council in Jerusalem, Peter proclaimed that God was at work through Jesus Christ by grace, extending faith to Jew and Gentile alike.

> And God, who knows the human heart, testified to them by giving them the Holy Spirit, just as he did to us; and in cleansing their hearts by faith he has made no distinction between them and us. Now therefore why are you putting God to the test by placing on the neck of the disciples a yoke that neither our ancestors nor we have been able to bear? On the contrary, we believe that we will be saved through the grace of the Lord Jesus, just as they will.
>
> (Acts15:8-11)

Human efforts would not bring salvation to the heart of either Jew or Gentile. The faith history of the Jews themselves had proved this. Grace alone would bring salvation, a salvation given to both Jew and Gentile and received through faith.

The Council at Jerusalem eventually decided to send the Gentile Christians a letter of peace through which they joined them in a common faith in Jesus Christ. They asked of the Gentile Christians only the essentials of what they understood to be necessary for clean and righteous living before God—that they abstain from what had been sacrificed to idols and from blood, and from what is strangled, and from fornication (Acts 15:28-29). These essentials the Jewish Christians also accepted unto themselves, becoming free of the belief of generations that somehow they could save themselves through good works. It was a moment of divine grace for all.

Faith in Jesus is in and of itself a gift. It is the work of the Holy Spirit as God reaches out to the world through grace. Today the Christian church is well established as a global church, but this does not keep it from struggling. Like the early Jewish Christians, the Christian church of this third millennium continues to often impose its own limited perspective of Christian faith to the exclusion of persons.

As a third-generation Christian, it has taken me a lifetime to regain the goodness of my Mexican culture because some Christian mission perspectives deemed my culture to be pagan and unpleasing to God. I fear that others of my culture have been unable to fully surrender their lives to Christ, not because of unbelief, but because of the institutional church that, not unlike the early church, does not know how to allow the church to be Christ's church, a church that beckons and welcomes the great diversity of God's people.

In the United States the Christian church, more often than not, identifies with the middle- and upper-classes of society. The poor may be objects of the outreach work of the church, but are rarely seen in the life and decision-making processes of the church. There are persons of homosexual orientation among us who join Christians everywhere in professing faith in Christ through word and deed yet the doors of many churches remain closed to them. I yearn for a day when, with Peter, the church will proclaim, "And God, who knows the human heart, testified to them by giving them the Holy Spirit, just as he did to us; and in cleansing their hearts by faith he has made no distinction between them and us....we believe that we will be saved through the grace of the Lord Jesus, just as they will" (Acts 15:8-9, 11). We are reminded that the ancient story of Christian faith holds up for us a glorious picture of a people rich and poor, Jew and Gentile, men and women, redeemed by grace who lived in community and to whom "day by day the Lord added to their number those who were being saved" (Acts 2:47b). So how are we to address faith in Christ Jesus today?

The Letter to the Hebrews contains what has become a classic statement about our understanding of Christian faith. Hebrews states, "Now faith is the assurance of things hoped for, the conviction of things not seen" (Hebrews 11:1). Hebrews then proceeds to trace the faith experiences of the patriarchs and other Israelite heroes: Abel, Enoch, Noah, Abraham, Moses, Gideon, Barak, Samson, Jephthah, David, Samuel, and the prophets. Finally, Hebrews turns to Jesus as "the pioneer and perfecter of our faith" (Hebrews 12:2a). In this way Hebrews chronologically traces the enduring faith of people who believed in God, but also, and perhaps more importantly, believed that God was at work in their lives redeeming and reclaiming the world for God's purposes. The faithful hoped for life, homeland, the blessing of descendants, and freedom from the tyranny of slavery and human sin. They hoped in the sure confidence that God was faithful. According to Hebrews, the faithful find the fulfillment of all their hopes in Jesus Christ. Faith is hope—hope in God who is always faithful. Faith is thus not only a set of beliefs, but also a relationship with the One who inspires faith.

John Wesley, the founder of Methodism, spoke of faith as the response of persons to God who is faithful in human history. Even then faith is a gift from God that can only be received with great thanksgiving. Building on the words of Ephesians 2:8, Wesley wrote in his sermon, *Salvation by Faith*:

> If we sinful people find favor with God, it is only from the fullness of his grace that we receive blessing after blessing. If God favors us by pouring fresh blessings upon us—yes, the greatest of all blessings, which is salvation—we can only say, "Thanks be unto God for his indescribable gift!" and so it is that God demonstrated his love for us in this: While we were still sinners, Christ died for us. "For by grace you have been saved through faith, and this is not your own doing; it is the gift of God." Grace is the source and faith the condition of our salvation.[1]

Wesley is careful to explain that the faith of which he speaks is not just any kind of faith, but rather a "saving" faith. Saving faith is different from the faith of heathens, Wesley declares. While heathens may acknowledge that God exists, saving faith leads the believer to a life that is pleasing to God. In Scripture demons hold intellectual knowledge of God even to the degree that they express awareness of the fact that Jesus is the Son of God (Matthew 8:29), yet they do not submit to his authority over their lives, resisting his touch of healing and redemption. The demons believe only that Jesus has the power to torment them, viewing him as enemy rather than as friend. Wesley further states that not even the faith of the apostles prior to Jesus' resurrection is sufficient. While the apostles followed Jesus in life at great sacrifice to themselves, they did not yet fully understand "the necessity of Christ's death, its merit, and the power of his Resurrection."[2] For Wesley, saving grace is trust in Christ:

> [It is] more than an intellectual assent to the entire gospel of Christ. It also means a complete reliance

on the blood of Christ; it is full trust in the merits of his life, death, and Resurrection. Saving faith is a resting upon Christ as our atonement and our life. A savior who gave himself for us and lives in us. The result of saving faith is uniting with Christ, and adhering firmly to him "who became for us wisdom from God, and righteousness and sanctification and redemption." In a word, Christ is our salvation.[3]

In the Gospel According to John, chapter 20, we find Mary Magdalene at the tomb of Jesus on that first day of the consummation of Christian faith. We watch expectantly as right before our eyes Mary Magdalene goes from following Jesus to understanding and receiving the power of Christ's resurrection for her life. And what a gift to become the first bearer of the mighty good news! There is no doubt that Mary Magdalene believed in the healing power of Jesus for he had healed her from the demons that had possessed her life. She obviously loved Jesus for in the horror of that dreadful place and hour she had come alone to give expression to her devotion to Jesus. Hers was a persevering love, for even as Peter and John came and went from tomb to home she remained at the place of Jesus' burial. Mary's love of Jesus was unselfish.

As Jesus appears, unrecognizable to her human eyes, Mary, thinking that Jesus is the gardener, pleads with him, "Sir, if you have carried him away, tell me where you have laid him, and I will take him away" (John 20:15b). How true the proverb, "Love knows no load." None of these attributes, however, gain for Mary that incredible gift of faith in a resurrected Lord. Rather it is the power of God at work in Jesus that faithfully and lovingly reveals to Mary that Jesus is alive. Without God's merciful action in first resurrecting Christ Jesus and then revealing this truth to her, Mary would never have been able to confess that she had seen the Lord, not as a dead corpse in a cold tomb, but as her living Savior bringing comfort to her grieving heart. This Mary proclaimed to the disciples and proclaims to us to this day. Mary Magdalene went from the empty tomb to the disciples, sharing with them in all faith that she had seen the Risen, Living Lord. She carried with her no proof of this incredible witness other than the conviction of her heart. Other hearts were not so easily convinced.

After hearing Mary Magdalene's witness, the disciples continued to live in fear behind locked doors (John 20:19). Jesus appeared to them showing them his hands and his side and then they "saw the Lord" (John 20:20), believing that the one before them was the Risen Lord. Thomas, however, having been absent during this appearance of the Lord was not to be convinced by the simple telling of the experience of those who had seen the Risen Lord. "Unless I see the mark of the nails in his hands, and put my finger in the mark of the nails and my hand in his side, I will not believe," (John 20:25b) is the statement that gained Thomas the descriptive title of "Doubting Thomas."

Jesus in his mercy appeared again to the disciples in the presence of Thomas and invited Thomas to place his finger in the wounds of his hands and to reach out and touch the gash in his side. As Thomas reached out to verify by human touch that the one before him truly was the crucified Jesus now resurrected, Jesus exhorted him not to doubt but believe (John 20:26-27). In that moment of mystery touched by human hands, Thomas was able to confess his faith as he exclaimed, "My Lord and my God!" (John 20:28). But then Thomas was faced by the challenge that has confronted believers of every generation. "Jesus said to him, 'Have you believed because you have seen me? Blessed are those who have not seen and yet have come to believe'" (John 20:29). Faith is indeed a matter of the heart encountered by the touch of the Holy Spirit.

In the *New and Enlarged Handbook of Christian Theology*, by

Donald W. Musser and Joseph L. Price, we find the following definition of faith from a Christian perspective:

> In Christian thought generally, the mystery and miracle of God's love in Christ, confirmed in the heart of the believer by the Holy Spirit, was the basis of trust and confidence that constituted the disposition of the believer who had known and continued to live by the redemptive reality and promise of God, even when it seemed that God did not always appear to be present.[4]

Shortly after the crucifixion, death, and resurrection of Christ Jesus, the early Christians would be challenged not only by the call to trust and confide in the Risen Lord, but also by the hostility and persecution of a world that continues to this day in unbelief. Not only did they have to find ways to carry and nurture their faith in their daily living, but often they were forced to defend their faith, sometimes even with their lives. Fortunately, the Holy Spirit accompanied them, giving them the assurance of the presence of Christ Jesus, especially in the hour of their greatest need. The day my grandmother Sofia died I knew that it was the Holy Spirit confirming in my heart that death would not have the last word because of Christ Jesus. Even though I suffered through moments when I doubted that God was present, the Holy Spirit kept nudging me back to that place of heartfelt faith. In the greater scheme of Christian faith, my experience is but a minor witness to faith and the sustaining grace of the Holy Spirit.

As a story of incredible faith and the sustaining grace of the Holy Spirit, the story of the early Christian martyrs, Perpetua and Felicity, has always amazed and moved me. Perpetua was a second-century young woman of some wealth from Carthage, North Africa, who, at the age of twenty-two, became a Christian martyr along with Felicity, her servant. Though nothing is known of her husband, it is known that Perpetua had a newborn son and a devoted father when she and Felicity, along with several male companions, were imprisoned for defying the prohibition against conversion to Christianity. When she was brought to trial for her crime of Christian faith the authorities urged Perpetua to reconsider her faith decision out of care for her aging father and her child. Perpetua's response to the court was the clear and simple declaration, "I am a Christian." It was not that Perpetua had lost a mother's love for her child, but rather that she understood that the prospect of dying for Christ was part of the cost of her discipleship. As for her father, she was saddened by the fact that his lack of faith in Christ Jesus did not allow him to understand her ability to rejoice in her imminent passion.

When Perpetua and Felicity were arrested for their crime of having become Christians, Felicity was eight months pregnant. She suffered not for herself but at the thought that the baby in her womb would be afflicted. After a night of prayer, however, she gave birth to a daughter and, like Perpetua, was able to leave her child in the hands of Christian friends.

Perpetua and Felicity were sentenced to the horrible fate of fighting wild animals in the amphitheater. Church history records that they were taken into the amphitheater and forced to remove their clothing, a shocking moment for the spectators who could then see that they were but very young women, and one with breasts bearing all the signs of having recently birthed a baby. They were allowed to cover their bodies as a savage cow was released into the amphitheater with them. Though spared by the horns of the cow and thrown about, they survived this phase of their ordeal. Finally, a swordsman was ordered to behead them, but being inexperienced he struggled with the task. The story of how Perpetua then helped the swordsman by directing the sword to her own neck became a word of encouragement to other Christians that faith does sustain in the midst of persecution and even cruel death. Perpetua and Felicity could have denied their faith in Christ Jesus. Immediately before being taken into the amphitheater they were given that opportunity but Perpetua, speaking for both, is recorded to have said,

> For this cause came we willingly unto this, that our liberty might not be obscured. For this cause have we devoted our lives.[5]

It is also recorded that before being beheaded, Perpetua and Felicity were observed by all giving each other a holy kiss, a sign that the separation of mistress and servant dictated by the social requirements of that day and age had been erased by their common faith in Christ Jesus. Perpetua and Felicity represent Christians of every generation, who, having known the love of God through Christ Jesus, have thus lived and died with the full trust and confidence that they are not alone, for God, who has acted decisively in Christ Jesus to save the world, is with us. They are persons who have known of what Paul spoke when he wrote to the Romans saying:

> Therefore, since we are justified by faith, we have peace with God through our Lord Jesus Christ, through whom we have obtained access to this grace in which we stand; and we boast in our hope of sharing the glory of God. And not only that, but we boast in our sufferings, knowing that suffering produces endurance, and endurance produces character, and character produces hope, and hope does not disappoint us, because God's love has

been poured into our hearts through the Holy
Spirit that has been given to us.

(Romans 5:15)

Such Christians can still be found today.

Not so long ago I had the good fortune of traveling to
Cochabamba, Bolivia, with a church delegation visiting an assembly of Methodist churches from Latin America and the Caribbean.
During this assembly we heard stories of deep faith in the midst of
great struggle. Cuban Christians spoke of how the controlling
forces of a secular and, some would say, atheistic society, had
begun to crumble, giving way to the expression of Christian faith,
a faith that many in the world had assumed dead in Cuba.
Christians from Honduras shared how God was enabling them to
plant an emerging church in this poverty-stricken country. While
there were little to no material resources for such work, God's Holy
Spirit was touching and transforming lives nonetheless. We visited
a church under construction, physically and missionally. With a
half-completed church building, the members of this congregation
had already established a clinic to care for the poor, as well as
organized a strong team of lay evangelists whose faith commitment
led them to care for the needs of the souls and bodies of their
neighbors. Their clear witness was that faith had led them to a
deep and passionate love of God and neighbor. As we came to
know the members of this congregation we realized that they were
themselves materially poor, yet understood themselves to be rich in
the mercies of Christ Jesus. It was a moving faith experience made
that much more meaningful by a most unexpected encounter with
a young boy of faith in the city's marketplace, the *mercado*.

We were approaching the last days of our visit and we had
not had an opportunity to purchase those gifts that our fami-

lies and co-workers were expecting us to bring home to them. So we skipped an afternoon session, hailed a taxi, and headed for the mercado. In the center of the city we were delivered to the very door of the mercado, a large structure that covered an entire city block. Moving from bright sunlight into the cavernous structure we found ourselves blinded by its darkness. Soon, though, our eyes adjusted to what was only partial darkness. As our eyes became accustomed to the gray of the interior of the mercado we could see that it was a maze of hallways lined by hundreds of tiny stalls filled with the beautiful textures and colors of Bolivian artwork, the scent of native flowers, spices, and perfumes, and the warmth of Bolivian hospitality.

I found myself wandering up and down the hallways of the mercado, still adjusting to the lack of light to illuminate my way, unable to choose what, among all the wonderful things before me, I would purchase to take home. Then, just as my eyes were becoming accustomed to the limited light, I came across a small stall that threw my eyes into confusion again for light shone forth with shocking brightness. As I refocused my eyes I could see that there was a small hole in the roof right above this stall that was allowing light from the sun to pour in, but to this day I am convinced that light was also emanating from the small child seated in the middle of the stall.

The child was a young boy of no more than ten years of age. I do not remember what he was selling, but I do remember what he was doing. Seated on an old crate he was reading a very large book resting on a round, makeshift table. From its bent and beaten pages I could tell that it was a well-read book. As I looked closer I could see that its pages were highlighted by a rainbow of colors giving emphasis to some of its sections. I stood in utter silence, not wanting to disturb the child in his reading, conscious of a sense of sacredness in the moment. The child seemed oblivious to my presence and I knew instinctively that it was not because of my efforts to be still in order not to disturb him, but rather his total focus on what he was reading. I leaned ever so slightly towards the boy and realized that he was reading the Bible. Very gently I said to him, "That is a good book you are reading." Without ever taking his eyes away from his Bible the boy responded with a firmness that surprised me, "It is the *best* book in the world." I found myself smiling and then I said to him, "I am a Christian too."

Upon hearing my confession of faith that little boy whose face I had not even yet fully seen turned to me, giving me a smile that immediately touched my heart for it was filled with both an innocent, tender love and an exuberant joy. Jumping to his feet he came straight over to me, enfolding me in a full, unconditional embrace and declaring that it was so good to meet another Christian. This child's declaration of his faith in Christ Jesus and his willingness to accept my own declaration of faith so moved me that I began to weep. All at once I was overwhelmed by the feeling that I knew him, loved him, and was bound to him by our mutual faith in the Lord of all life. As we parted from each other this young Christian encouraged me to be faithful and to pray that he would likewise be faithful in his life. I no longer remember his name and am regretful that I did not write it down somewhere to help my forgetful mind. My heart, however, will never forget him for he strengthened my faith and reminded me that we do not live our faith alone, but rather in the company of others whose hearts have also been touched by Christ Jesus and whose lives have been forever changed by Christ's gift of redeeming grace.

2 Faith in Jesus Over the Generations

As a child sitting in church next to my beloved grandmother Sofia, I took great pride in reciting the Apostles' Creed. It made me feel as if I was truly a member of the Christian church universal. I was proud to be able to state what I believed. Even more, I wanted to share Christ Jesus with the entire world, and the Apostles' Creed gave me the words to share my faith when I was just beginning to learn how to give witness to the saving grace of Christ in my life.

Believing in Jesus stirs our hearts to wanting to share the good news with all people. The early Christians were passionate about proclaiming faith in Christ Jesus. As the years passed after the crucifixion, death, and resurrection of Jesus, preserving the faith, as well as helping disciples articulate the faith, led to the development of Christian doctrine. Christologies, or understandings of the nature, person, and work of Jesus Christ, were some of the earliest Christian doctrines.

The First Letter of Paul to the Thessalonians is the first proclamation of the gospel in written form. Written about 50 C.E., I Thessalonians provides us with some of the earliest Christian creedal formulas:

- "his Son from Heaven, whom he raised from the dead—Jesus, who rescues us from the wrath that is coming" (1:10);

- "For since we believe that Jesus died and rose again, even so, through Jesus, God will bring with him those who have died" (4:14);

- "For God has destined us not for wrath but for obtaining salvation through our Lord Jesus Christ, who died for us, so that whether we are awake or asleep we may live with him" (5:9-10).

These earliest of Christian creedal formulas helped shape the creeds we use today to proclaim our faith in Christ Jesus. Seeking to strengthen their faith Paul wrote to the Christians of Thessalonica to remind them in whom they believed. They believed in the resurrected Son of God who would rescue them from the coming wrath. Those who believe in Jesus will live with him in life and in death. Throughout all of his letters Paul strives to help the early Christians affirm in whom they believe. Paul's fervent and tireless witness arises from the belief that Christ Jesus is able to do for humanity what neither law nor religious observances can accomplish. In Christ Jesus alone is the radical salvation that reconciles humanity with God, bringing abundant life to all who believe.

The growth of the early church brought together persons of varying experiences and understandings of Jesus' life, ministry, crucifixion, death, and resurrection. It soon became clear that some of these understandings threatened the very core of the Christian faith. This led the church to the very serious task of clearly and faithfully articulating the Christian faith.

Gnosticism, a belief that spiritual matters can be fully explained through knowledge, became an early threat to Christianity. Gnostics did not believe that God had revealed God's self to the people of Israel and thus they rejected the Old Testament. They denied the true humanity of Christ. For them Christ was divine and only appeared to be human. Thus Jesus did not die on the cross, he only *appeared* to be crucified on the cross. Gnostics also did not believe in the kingdom of God or the end of time for in their historical perspective history had no goal. Church historian Martin Marty describes the Gnostics and their relationship with the early Christians and Christian faith:

> The Gnostics scorned ordinary Christians who walked by faith: they walked by sight, they knew, they had access to secret bodies of knowledge.[1]

Two forms of Gnosticism were particularly difficult, Docetism and Adoptionism. Docetic Gnostics believed that Jesus was only divine spirit and that his human body was but a mere illusion. Irenaeus, an early church father, reported a version of Docetic heresy that declared that Christ had not died because Jesus had not died. These heretics believed that the one who had been crucified was not Jesus but Simon of Cyrene who helped Jesus carry the cross to Golgatha. These Docetists were convinced that, while Simon of Cyrene had died on the cross, Jesus had stood by watching and laughing at the Jews in their delusions![2] Docetic Gnosticism brought into question how believers in such a Savior were to behave. If the body was unimportant as seemed the case in Docetic thought, then what Christians did with their bodies was unimportant as long as their minds were focused on higher, divine thoughts. In Romans 6:1-12 Paul appears to be arguing against this erroneous Gnostic perspective of the nature of Christ and the community that believes in him.

> What then are we to say? Should we continue in
> sin in order that grace may abound?
> By no means! How can we who died to sin,
> go on living in it?…
> So you also must consider yourselves
> dead to sin and alive to God, in Christ Jesus.
> Therefore, do not let sin exercise dominion in your
> mortal bodies, to make you obey their passions.
> (Romans 6:1-2, 11-12)

Adoptionists believed that Jesus was not of a divine nature, but rather an extremely good person whose goodness so moved God that God adopted him as God's own son. This thinking stood in direct opposition to the doctrine of Incarnation; that in Jesus, God took the form of human flesh and lived among us. Gnostics also denied the final Resurrection, eternal life in the body. The Apostles' Creed evolved as a rejection of Gnosticism. This historic creed also stood in direct opposition to the doctrine of another heretical group, Marcionites.

Marcion was a wealthy shipowner from Sinope in Pontus. He was also the son of a bishop who excommunicated him from the church for immoral behavior. Even as one excommunicated, Marcion did not absent himself from the church. Instead he organized a separate community of faith that became what church historians register as the greatest threat to the Christian church in latter half of the second century. Marcion's central belief was that the Christian gospel was a gospel of love to the absolute exclusion of law.[3] He believed that the body and the affairs of the world were evil and thus that Jesus had only *appeared* to be human rather than being the incarnation of God. Believing that the body is evil he did not therefore believe in the resurrection of the body. Furthermore, he did not believe that the world was created by God, but rather by a demiurge, or subordinate of God, sometimes regarded as the originator of evil.

In addition, Marcion believed that the God of the Old Testament was not the equivalent of the Father of Jesus, but rather an inferior being. He set aside the Old Testament arguing that it represented the book of a lesser god. Marcion compiled a New Testament canon that took parts of the Gospel According to Luke, and pieces of the letters of Paul, focusing on those writings that promoted love. By working on his own canon, Marcion also forced the early church fathers to determine what would be included in the New Testament canon.[4] Marcion was not the only one to challenge Christian faith. Arius and Nestorius also challenged the faith.

The Arian controversy challenged the church to consider the divinity of Jesus. Arius, a presbyter in Alexandria, believed that though the Word had become incarnate in Jesus, and had preexisted before the rest of creation, Jesus was not "God of very God," but rather the first of all creatures. According to Arius, only the Father is eternal, while the Son or Word is not. Those who opposed Arius argued that Christ is the true God, and that the reason we can call Christ our Savior is that he is God. The Arian controversy was settled at the Council of Nicea in 325 C.E. The Council declared that Jesus was both human and divine, and issued the Nicene Creed. Those who disagreed were labeled Arian heretics.

Nestorius, a fifth-century monk from Antioch and the patriarch of Constantinople from 428-431 C.E., struggled with other aspects of the nature of Jesus, namely the fact that some were saying that Mary was the Mother of God. He argued that Mary had given birth to the human Jesus not the divine. Saying that Mary had birthed God undermined, in Nestorius' opinion, the human nature of Christ. For Nestorius the human and the divine natures of Jesus were conjoined and acted as one but were not one in the sense of being a single person. Under the leadership of Pope Leo I the matter was addressed at the Council of Chalcedon in 451 C.E.

The Council of Chalcedon recognized in Christ two natures without confusion, change, division, or separation in one person and subsistence. The incarnate Christ was a single person, at once God and man. Though the controversy stirred by Nestorius would continue over the next two centuries, the Council of Constantinople in 681 C.E. would reaffirm the Council of Chalcedon's decision about the nature of Christ Jesus.[5] At the beginning of this controversy Protestants tended to assume that it was an issue of Mariology (the worship of Mary), but what the early church was trying to understand was what it meant for God to be incarnate in Jesus, living among us, suffering alongside us, and even dying on a cross for our salvation. The early Christians did affirm that Mary is the Mother of God or the bearer of God. Followers of Nestorius survive today in Kurdistan under the name of Assyrian Christians, also known as the Church of the East.

While this quick review of some of the major controversies about the nature of Christ Jesus does not do justice to the efforts of Christians over generations to be faithful to their understanding of the meaning of the life, ministry, crucifixion, death, and resurrection of Christ, it hopefully raises an awareness of the complexity and importance of the effort. In summary, the Christian church ultimately affirmed that Jesus is the long-awaited Messiah proclaimed by the prophets of the Old Testament and that Jesus is both human and divine; the incarnation of God, yet also a human being who has experienced our human weaknesses, sufferings, temptations, and even death. The encounter of the early Christians with the Risen Lord and their witness through the power of the Holy Spirit led the Christian church to proclaim that God had resurrected Jesus from the cruel cross of death to life. Jesus is Christ, Lord and Savior of the world. Death is the ultimate consequence of human sin, and thus the Resurrection is understood as Jesus Christ's overcoming the penalty of sin in the world and the redeeming of creation to a right relationship with God and with all creatures.

Through the outpouring of the Holy Spirit on the day of Pentecost, Christians came to know themselves as bound together with each other and with Christ Jesus their head. Thus the concept of Christians being the body of Christ Jesus began to be articulated and lived out in the fellowship of Christians. The demands of mission and ministry gave way to the organization of the church, and while Christians strive to faithfully live and serve as disciples of Christ Jesus in the world, we await Christ's second coming in glory when he will "judge the living and the dead and his kingdom will have no end."[6]

In *An Introduction to Christian Theology*, authors Justo L. González and Zaida Maldonado Pérez, help us to understand the great significance of the church's affirmations about Jesus. In order to understand why it is that Christians claim Jesus as Christ, Lord and Savior of the world, González and Pérez describe for us the saving work of Christ through an analysis of the historic theories of Atonement. Atonement simply defined is the making of amends or reparation for an offense. Thus Jesus makes amends or reparation for our human sin. Throughout the history of Christian faith several explanations have been offered about how Jesus accomplishes such Atonement in behalf of humanity. Turning to Anselm of Canterbury in the twelfth century González and Pérez summarize the theological concept of Jesus as the one who makes payment for sin.

According to Anselm, sin is an injury against God's honor, and therefore whoever sins is in debt to God. In the feudal society in which Anselm lived, when someone's honor was injured, it was thought that it was necessary to repair the damage by honoring that person in ways that would counterbalance the injury itself. In such cases, the importance of the injury depended on the dignity of the offended party, whereas the value of the honor rendered depended on the dignity of the one offering it. Thus, an apparently minor injury to the honor of a monarch was a grave fault; but if a person of low standing wished to honor that same monarch, this would be very difficult, for the value of this person's act would be measured in terms of his or her social position, and that of the king. If then sin is understood as a debt that sinful humanity has contracted by injuring the honor of the infinite God, such debt can never be paid, for the injury is infinite, and the sinner is not.[7]

Anselm's theory of Atonement thus led him to the conclusion that if sin is of a human nature, reparation for it must be rendered by a human agent. However, since the offense of human sin was against an infinite God, then an infinite payment was necessary. Thus God who is the only one who can make an infinite payment had to take human form in Christ Jesus in order to make things right.[8] Anselm's theory of Atonement is the one most commonly held by Protestants and Catholics even today, but González and Pérez find both strengths and weaknesses in it.

On the one hand they argue that this theory of Atonement does paint a vivid picture of the depth of human sin. Human sin is so great it affects God and leads God in divine and loving mercy to sacrifice to save humanity from the power of sin over life. On the other hand it also paints a picture of God as vengeful, petty, and determined to defend his honor until every last offense is paid for. If this is who God is then what is the purpose of Jesus' life of mercy and healing, of justice and peace? Is God a god of wrath and Jesus a loving Savior? González and Pérez offer the insight that through the crucifixion, death, and resurrection of Jesus Christ, humanity and all of creation are set free not from the demands of a god of wrath, but from the power of Satan. Referring back to other early Christian writers they state:

> As a result of sin humankind became enslaved to Satan, who was not ready to grant its freedom except at a very high price. Such was the price paid by Jesus on the cross.
>
> The advantage of this old understanding is that it is not God, but Satan, who demands the sacrifice of Jesus, and therefore there is no tendency to establish a contrast between the Father and the Son regarding their love of humanity.[9]

Gonzáles and Pérez hold up for our consideration three other Atonement theories about the saving action of Christ Jesus that are important for our study: Jesus as a saving example, Jesus as conqueror, and Jesus as the head of a new humanity.

First credited to Abelard, a contemporary of Anselm of Canterbury, the Atonement theory of Jesus as a saving example argues that humanity is moved to repentance of sin by the loving nature of Christ. As we see Christ suffer on the cross with a love so great that it even forgives those who crucify him, we are convicted of our sin, turn away from sin, and choose to lead holy lives.

Abelard was convinced that the alienation from God did not so much affect God as it affected us as our rebellion distanced us further and further from God.

Rightly so, González and Pérez argue that Abelard's theory fails to consider the fullness of the power of sin. Secondly, they argue that Abelard's theory makes of Jesus just another good example and if Jesus is but a good example, then humanity can find other good examples for its salvation. While Abelard's Atonement theory may sound both distant and limited, it was widely accepted in the not so distant nineteenth and twentieth centuries.

The Swedish theologian, Gustaf Aulén, was a principal proponent of the Atonement theory of Jesus as conqueror, though the early church theologian, Irenaeus of Lyon, was already formulating his own thoughts on this theory as early as the second century. Aulén proposes that Christ is the Savior of the world in that he frees humanity from its enslavement to Satan by defeating Satan. Thus the saving action of Jesus upon the cross is not so much a payment for the debts of humanity, but rather a liberating of humanity from Satan's oppressive grip. Sin's power over humanity is seen as overwhelming human capacity to overcome it and thus requiring divine intervention in order to conquer it. While González and Pérez find validity in Aulén's theory, they worry that modern society has lost a clear sense of the power of Satan over life and therefore is unable to clearly value the liberating significance of Christ's Atonement for human sin.

The fourth Atonement theory that González and Pérez encourage us to consider is that of Jesus as the head of a new humanity. First Corinthians 15:22 lays the foundation of this theory as it says, "for as all die in Adam, so all will be made alive in Christ." The New Testament understanding of this phrase is that Adam stands as the head of a sinful and fallen humanity while Jesus comes to restore humanity and become the new head of transformed humanity. Jesus is the Savior of the world inviting all persons to join him in his body, the church. In John 15 we find Jesus as Savior imaged as a vine with his disciples abiding in him as the branches of the true vine. While Jesus had to become human in order to become the new head of the new humanity, Jesus' divine power makes him able to give life to the branches, something that Adam is not able to do.

As head of a new humanity Christ's work does not end with his replacing of Adam. Christ's work continues through his body. As stated by González and Pérez,

> Whereas the old humanity is a body of sin and damnation whose head is Adam, the new humanity is a body of holiness and salvation whose head is Jesus.[10]

Jesus initiates the reign of God among us and invites us to live as members of his body and citizens of the reign of God. As United Methodists we claim Jesus by professing:

> ...the historic Christian faith in God, incarnate in Jesus Christ for our salvation and ever at work in human history in the Holy Spirit. Living in a covenant of grace under the Lordship of Jesus Christ, we participate in the first fruits of God's coming reign and pray in hope for its full realization on earth as in heaven.[11]

more open than creed

How do we come to believe this? According to Scripture it is by grace through faith. Writing to the Christians in Ephesus, Paul shares with them this biblical truth as he says, "For by grace you have been saved through faith, and this is not your own doing; it is the gift of God—" (Ephesians 2:8).

We understand grace to mean "the undeserved, unmerited, and loving action of God in human existence through the ever-present Holy Spirit."[12] John Wesley had a way of explaining grace that has guided Methodists not only in understanding the richness of God's grace, but also in living as disciples of Christ Jesus. Wesley describes the nature of God's grace through Christ as prevenient, justifying, sanctifying, and perfecting.

Earlier we spoke of prevenient grace as God's action of reaching out to us. In a fuller definition we would say that prevenient grace is the belief that even before we are aware of God's presence in our lives and in our hearts, God's spirit is at work convincing us of our need of God. We believe that God's prevenient grace surrounds all of humanity awakening within us a sense of our sin against God as well as a desire to be saved from sin and death. Prevenient grace moves us from sin to repentance and to faith.

Prevenient grace prepares us for justifying grace or the action of God that extends pardon and forgiveness of our sins through Jesus Christ. We believe that God's love comes to us as we confess our sin and seek to live in right relationship with God. This experience of conversion and the assurance of God's love for us comes to each of us in different ways. For some of us it comes in a dramatic moment of being convicted of our sin and our need of repentance. For others it comes gradually over time. All who receive God's justifying grace, however, experience a new beginning that leads to the living of faith through lives of holy love. We believe with the apostle Paul that we can be sure of this justifying grace in our lives because the very spirit of God bears witness to our spirit that we are children of God (Romans 8:16).

Justifying grace is but the beginning of a lifelong process of growing in grace. By the power of the Holy Spirit we are able to grow in our knowledge and love of God and in the love of our neighbor. The gift of God's grace through Jesus Christ continues to unfold in our lives as we strive to have the mind of Christ Jesus; as we strive for Christian perfection. With John Wesley we believe that by the grace of God we can be made perfect in this life. Wesley described this state of Christian perfection as a heart "habitually filled with the love of God and neighbor."[13]

Over the generations many have worked hard and diligently so that the Christian faith may be preserved and shared with integrity and faithfulness. As an inheritor of the work of God's people I found myself one day with my grandmother Sofia reciting the Apostles' Creed and remembering my first memory of God:

> I believe in God the Father Almighty,
> maker of heaven and earth;.
> and in Jesus Christ, his only Son, our Lord;
> who was conceived by the Holy Spirit,
> born of the Virgin Mary...[14]

My father, Juan Pablo, was a man who lived on the margins of the church. He became a Methodist when he fell in love with my mother and decided that he wanted to marry her. My grandmother Sofia would never have allowed her only daughter to marry someone who was not a member of the church. But my father lived his life outside the community of the church. What my father did do was find solitary ways to contribute to the life of the church such as the year he volunteered to prepare the Christmas tree for our church's sanctuary. With my mother's help I was able to locate this experience in my own faith journey. It is my earliest memory of an encounter with God. I was four years old and my sister Elizabeth was three. Hearing that our father was going to be preparing a Christmas tree we begged him to take us with him. My father gave in to our begging.

At our church father put up the biggest Christmas tree we had ever seen and then began to decorate it with huge, brightly colored balls, and streamers of glittering silver foil that wiggled through our fingers and sparkled to our delight. Elizabeth and I were in charge of decorating the lowest boughs of the tree. The fact that in my memory's eye I am able to see hundreds of tiny pieces of multicolored glass scattered all over the floor under the tree is probably a confirmation that we broke more decorations than we were able to place on the tree. It is nevertheless to this day one of my very favorite memories of Christmas. Laced through this favorite memory is the voice of my father telling us the Christmas story.

My father was never more gentle toward us than on that day. As we worked together he lovingly told us the Christmas story of how God had sent baby Jesus. Mary was the name of Jesus' mama and Joseph was his father. When the time had come for baby Jesus to be born, Mary and Joseph had no place where Mary could have the baby so baby Jesus was born in a stable among the animals. Growing up on a farm we could not imagine a baby in the stable. But God had gone ahead and sent baby Jesus to Mary and Joseph even in a stable so that we could know how much God loved us. The Christmas story connected us around that tree with a sense of purpose; others would also remember baby Jesus when they saw this tree we were preparing.

When the tree was decked-out with all the bulbs and lights it could hold, my father asked my sister and me to sit right in front of it in the very first pew in the sanctuary. He told us it would become dark in the sanctuary as he turned the lights off, but it would be just for a moment. He would be right back. When the lights went out in the sanctuary submerging us into immediate darkness my sister and I instinctively took the other's hand out of sheer fear of the darkness. Then we heard my father's footsteps as we felt him move in the darkness right by us. Suddenly, as my father plugged in the electrical cord of the Christmas tree's lights, we were transported from the fearful darkness to the extraordinarily comforting and lovely warmth of the light of the Christmas tree before us. It was the most beautiful thing I had ever seen, and as my sister and I sat in silent awe and amazement before this beautiful sight, I believed. I believed that God loved the world; loved all of us enough to send baby Jesus to a filthy, cold stable to be born among us so that we would know that God did love us. Through the dark moments of my life Jesus born of Mary has held my hand, illuminated my steps, spoken gently to my spirit, embraced me with the warmth of God's love. Yes, I do believe that God came down on Christmas, incarnate in the Christ Child, born of the Virgin Mary.

What a wonderful and lovely story the Christmas story is. As Christians we believe that the story is true; that on one splendid and wonder-filled night a virgin gave birth to a baby, that angels sang glorious songs of praise to God for the birth of this child of God, that shepherds witnessed it all, that the stars shone brightly in the midnight sky as a bright sign that God had appeared among mortals. In the darkness of life over 2,000 years ago, God came near to the world through the birth of the long-awaited Messiah, Jesus. God saw the suffering of persons and communities and all of creation through sin and oppression and made the divine decision to extend God's own grace and salvation to us. As persons of Christian faith, to this day we believe that the glorious story of Christmas day is true and faithful with deep and profound meaning for our lives. By faith we believe that God exists for we experience him in our souls and in our hearts when we open ourselves to God's presence.

As children it was easy for my sister and me to open our hearts to the wonder of a baby, ornaments of many colors, and bright, twinkling lights, but for my father it was another matter. On that day when we went to our church to set up the Christmas tree my father was estranged from the church because of his compulsive gambling. It was not that the church rejected him, but rather that he chose to absent himself from the church. I believe that he did not want to have to face his addiction to gambling for he felt powerless over it. I am sure that he carried a measure of shame about his gambling. On that afternoon as he told us the Christmas story though, there was a peace and a joy about my father that I would rarely see in him during the rest of his life. There was in that moment no doubt on his face or in his spirit, and it enabled us, his children, to also believe that God exists. God does exist, and we know it every time we open our hearts to God.

My father struggled all of his life with his addiction to gambling and a degree of self-hatred because he did not believe that he was worthy of love. He had grown up in a home where his mother had died when he was eleven years of age, and his father, perhaps out of his own despair, beat my father violently and frequently. If his father did not love him, then how could anyone love him, my father must have thought.

The good news of Christmas is that God who sends the baby Jesus does so because he loves us. And what a love it is! Who among us would give their child for sinners, or even for good people? Yet that is exactly what God does; he sends his Son with the foreknowledge that he would one day be crucified by a sinful and unbelieving world. But God does not count this as failure or as unwise, or even as wasteful of his Son's life, because of God's great love for us.

God cares about a world so alienated that God is willing to sacrifice the life of his only Son. It is the nature of God's love—unconditional, for his love extends to all people in all human circumstances; everlasting, for God who is love is eternal; faithful, for

God never forgets his own. My father was a beloved child of God, but he couldn't quite allow himself to believe it. What a difference it would have made if my father had truly believed that the story of Christmas he so lovingly shared with his children was a gift for his life as well. We are all beloved of God just as we are.

Our hope is found in God whose love we come to know through the birth of the Christ Child, God who has indeed made all things new (Revelation 21:5). What happened on that first Christmas was that God decided that it was time for God's very own self to intervene and save fallen and alienated humanity. God could see that because of humanity's sinful nature we could not overcome our sins on our own: the sins of hatred and self-centered-ness, the sins of greed and covetousness, the sins of self-idolatry and other idol-making, the sins of racism and sexism and homo-phobia. God could see that left to our own will we would never overcome our sins.

But there are also those who suffer because they are the vic-tims of the sins of others, persons and whole communities who suffer poverty and great oppression at the hands of those who consume more than their fair share. There are among us those who think they have the rights of gods and assume cruel power over others. Mary and Joseph were among the poor, oppressed by the ruling power of the Romans who thought themselves to be gods. Mary and Joseph were so poor that when they traveled to Bethlehem to be registered so that the oppressive Roman gov-ernment could tax them, they found no room for Mary to give birth to the baby Jesus. But the birth of the Christ Child in a manger among the poor and their animals was not just because Mary and Joseph were poor. In his power God could have made a special place for them for the birth of Jesus. God chooses the manger in a dirty stable as a sign that God has surely taken sides—God stands with the poor and the oppressed as he comes to destroy the power of sin over humanity and all of creation. In fact, Jesus is God in human flesh. Mary could see this happening as she proclaimed:

> He has brought down the
> powerful from their
> thrones,
> and lifted up the lowly;
> he has filled the hungry with
> good things,
> and sent the rich away empty.
>
> (Luke 1:52-53)

The poor and weak have good news proclaimed to them. God has looked down upon the world and heard the cry of God's peoples, has seen the affliction of those who suffer and been compassionate. God is with us. This does not mean that we are free to sin. God's hope is that God's compassionate stand with those who are oppressed will cause a change within us, a turning away from our sin so that we can be God's people of mercy, justice, and peace. In this way God's love is proclaimed also for the rich and powerful, and for those who fall into the sin of regarding their own lives more highly than the lives of others. Mercy, justice, and peace for all people will come for it is God's will for humanity. God has come and through Jesus initiated his reign among us making hope real for all of us. God in Jesus is the story of the Gospels.

What a difference faith in Jesus could make in the lives of our families, and neighborhoods, and in the world, if we decided in response to God's gift of the Christ Child to be God's people, a people who believe that the world can be made new and different, can be a loving and just place, a holy place where all persons are loved for we are all beloved of God. A place where on this day all persons feel the love of God, where all are fed, where the sick are cared for with great mercy, the elderly are honored and respected, the immigrant welcomed, and the rich share with the poor in ways that overcome greed and poverty. God gives us the strength of hope that this is all possible for God has transformed our world through Christ Jesus. As we receive Jesus into our lives we become hope for the world as our lives are transformed and we live as God's people in the world.

3 Whose Faith Counts?

Early in my life I felt God's claim upon my life. At the age of five I had a most unusual experience in which God confirmed in my heart that I would always live in God's house. I now believe that it was God's call to me to ordained ministry. It came to me on a rather ordinary day. Still watching for any and every opportunity to go to my beloved church, one day I again caught my father on one of his missions. He had agreed to replace the old vinyl flooring in our church's kindergarten classroom with fresh new vinyl. I offered to assist him and he accepted my offer.

The memory is so vivid in my spirit that I can still see and feel that old cracked, dirty vinyl as we pulled and scraped it off the floor. I can also smell the fresh scent of new, shiny vinyl. After my father had removed the old vinyl flooring, with my great help, of course, he told me that he had forgotten something in our car and would need to fetch it. He asked me to sit in the classroom and wait for him. I sat between the old and the new vinyl, already beginning to see how wonderful my own classroom was going to look with a fresh, new floor covering, when all of sudden I felt what my grandmother Sofia must have felt under the branches of the mesquite trees. I was overwhelmed by the intense feeling that I was not alone. I don't remember being afraid because I was sure that it was God present with me in that classroom holding me ever so tightly, embracing me with his love. In that encounter with the Holy I knew that I was home and that I would always live in God's house. At that young age I could not articulate what I had experienced but I did know the joy and the love of that sacred moment.

As a child and through my early teenage years I sought to understand my experience in that church kindergarten classroom. One day at a church youth rally I came to the understanding that God was calling me to be a pastor, and had been calling me since I was five years old. Now I was frightened and overwhelmed by this revelation of the Holy Spirit, but at the same time overjoyed by the clarity of God's presence and call that I felt within me. However, I was soon to discover that my joy was not shared by my father, my pastor, nor others in authority in my church. Even those who seemed affirming of my call were often patronizing. The negative assumption I began to encounter as I shared what I believed was my call to ordained ministry was that a woman could not possibly understand Scripture and thus could not be an effective proclaimer of the Holy Word. But every time someone lifted this objection I remembered my grandmother Sofia and my mother Rebecca who had taught me the faith and who had never hesitated in explaining the Holy Scriptures to me and others in our large extended family. Nor could I help remembering women of the Bible like Miriam, Deborah, the woman at the well of John's Gospel, the woman who dared to touch the hem of Jesus' cloak, Lois and Eunice—all great women of faith whose stories continue to inspire our faith today.

I have always understood my response to God's call in my life to ordained ministry as my best effort to live my faith in Christ Jesus. I have found it difficult over the years to have others question the validity of my call for I have experienced it as nothing less than a questioning of my faith. Now I must say that not everything I have experienced in my faith journey has turned out to be a God-led direction in my life. Human sin and weakness have led me down some lonely and forsaken roads. I also firmly believe that a call to ministry is best understood under the care of the church. Yet the reasons given to me for why I could not serve God in the ordained ministry did not satisfy me. Most of all they left me wondering about whose faith counts.

My years in seminary helped me to understand that the conflict I experienced with those who did not understand, much less accept, my call to ordained ministry as a response to faith in Jesus was more than just a personal matter. I came to learn that we lived in a culture of Christian faith that over the generations has had little room for women and their leadership in general, and even less room for the faith and gifts of women of color.

The earliest Christologies assumed a patriarchal perspective of Holy Scripture and Christian tradition. The early church was dominated by males, in both Eastern and Western traditions. Over the generations of Christian faith North American and Northern European white male theologians have asserted that the context in which we come to know Jesus is universal, and that knowing Jesus is an objective enterprise. Furthermore, they have audaciously presented a white male interpretation of Scripture as the only possible objective interpretation of who Jesus is. Thus, they have determined that the white male experience of God is the one true, universal, and objective understanding of the divine. Therefore, in this line of reasoning, women and men of color by the very essence of who they are cannot fully articulate Christian faith. I do not believe that white males have approached theology thinking that they would exclude women and people of color. Rather, they have worked as society has expected them to work, as those with the authority and the privilege to define what is acceptable and what is not in the defining of faith and its expression.

The theological thinking of some brave Christians of the last century, however, gifted us with fresh new thoughts about Jesus and his presence in our daily lives. Liberation theologies from the pits of human suffering have enabled us to see the face of Jesus in the poor. Feminist, Womanist, and Mujerista theologies have nudged our hearts to consider dimensions of God known through the eyes of women. In addition, theologies from the contexts of Asia, Africa, Latin America, and the Pacific Islands have contributed to new understandings of Jesus. These theologies have made us aware of the importance of social context. Jesus does indeed meet us where we are, cares about our struggles, and yearns for our well-being.

In 1970, just a few years before I entered seminary, three major theologians added their voice, their critique, and their perspective to Christian theology. Working independently of each other, in three different parts of the American continent, Gustavo Gutiérrez, James H. Cone, and Rosemary Radford Ruether wrote theological texts with very similar titles. In Peru, Father Gustavo Gutiérrez wrote *A Theology of Liberation.* In New York City, Professor James H. Cone wrote *A Black Theology of Liberation.* And in Chicago, Dr. Rosemary Radford Ruether wrote *Liberation Theology.* These three texts changed forever the nature of the theological discussion for Christian faith.

Rosemary Radford Ruether brought forth in her writing the first complete systematic theological work from a feminist perspective. Throughout her book she challenged patriarchy, the institutional and systematic valuing of men as inherently better than women. In a religious patriarchal system God is viewed as patriarch, and men in their maleness are assumed to be the best human representation of God. Women, therefore. cannot represent God for they are considered inferior in both image and ability. Radford Ruether rightly unmasks patriarchy's negation and trivialization of women. She encourages women to affirm their bodies, their faith, and their spirituality. By writing from a woman's faith perspective, Dr. Radford Ruether helped to create a space for the faith experience and expression of women.

In his book *A Black Theology of Liberation*, James H. Cone forced the church and the theological world to reconsider how it approached its understanding of God, and the meaning of salvation in Christ. Speaking from the pain and oppression of the black community in the US, he challenged Christian theologians everywhere by his bold declaration that any message not related to the liberation of the poor in a society is not Christ's message. Any theology that is indifferent to the theme of liberation is not Christian theology. The social location of Cone's contribution to the theological conversation about the meaning of salvation as liberation from all that enslaves a person and limits God's purposes for all of humanity, was the black revolution in the US, but he transcended the American black revolution by speaking a word of hope for those oppressed everywhere. As Radford Ruether had done for women, Cone gave voice to the faith understanding of African Americans, an understanding that enriched the faith of the church universal.

Not unlike the basis of James H. Cone's book, Gustavo Gutiérrez's theological work was inspired by the suffering and hopes of the poor of Latin America. As a Peruvian Roman Catholic priest Father Gutiérrez daily saw the great human struggles of his parishioners as well as the social and political structures that seemed indifferent to the poor. He lamented that all too often the institutional church was just as indifferent. In his groundbreaking book *A Theology of Liberation*, Gutiérrez insists that if we truly love our neighbor we will take concrete steps to address the needs of our neighbor. Gutiérrez calls this the praxis of faith, or the active practice of what we claim to believe. Salvation through Jesus, according to Gutiérrez, is the liberation from all forms of sin including the sins of injustice and oppression. Only then can persons be in full communion with God and each other. Gutiérrez was critical of sociopolitical and economic powers that abused persons for their own gain, and was critical of the Christian church for its complacency in responding to the struggles of oppressed communities. It could be documented in fact that throughout history the Christian church was guilty of moments in its life when it had aligned itself with the secular power structures that had oppressed communities. Gutiérrez argues that sin and salvation are concrete social acts, rather than abstract concepts, and that what is most important in a Christian's faith journey is the practice of one's belief. Faith praxis, according to Gutiérrez, is more important than theological reflection, and theological reflection is never authentic without praxis. Through his theological contribution Gutiérrez challenged the faith of the wealthy and powerful and led the Christian poor to interpret their own faith through the perspective that central to Jesus' life and message was their liberation.

So whose faith counts? What I discovered through the study of Radford Ruether, Cone, and Gutiérrez, along with the study of the works of white male theologians like Karl Barth, Paul Tillich, and Reinhold Niebuhr, is that everyone's voice is important to the theological dialogue. Reflecting and speaking truthfully, carefully, and lovingly from those social contexts in which God has placed us, guided by Holy Scripture and the Holy Spirit, we can all help the church and each other to be more faithful disciples of Jesus Christ. Those who have taken the risk of speaking out about their faith have empowered the life and ministry of the church, the body of Jesus Christ.

One of the empowering contributions that emerged from these new perspectives in Christology was the suggestion that the pictures of Christ that have dominated church history were, in all probability, incorrect, and surely incomplete. Jesus did not look like the blond-haired, blue-eyed landowners of my childhood. He looked much more like the poor who picked the crops; like my uncles and my brothers. He was indeed like the lover in the Song of Solomon:

> I am black and beautiful, O daughters of Jerusalem, like the tents of Kedar, like the curtains of Solomon. Do not gaze at me because I am dark, because the sun has gazed on me.
>
> (Song of Solomon 1:5-6a)

These notions had already been explored in the preaching of several Latino and black pastors but, for the first time they were in print and were being discussed in seminaries and church consultations. Cecil "Chip" Murray, who served African Methodist Episcopal churches until his retirement in 2004, often remarked when dealing with the text of the escape of the Holy Family to Egypt, "If Jesus and his family had been light-skinned, Herod would have found them very easily in Egypt. You can't hide vanilla in chocolate!" How true this is, and only a person of color can fully articulate this truth with all of the human vulnerability it points to. Some find this thinking threatening for it means that some may know dimensions of the life and humanity of Jesus that others may not know quite as intimately. I would rather view this reality as a sign of our need of each other as we strive to know Jesus.

Robert McAfee Brown, a North American theologian, did not see the images of Christ that were being lifted up by Latin American, feminist, and African-American theologians as disturbing. Rather, he found them enlightening and affirming of his earlier pastoral instincts. In his memoirs he tells of a Christmas function he held during his short time as a chaplain in the Navy in 1946:

> At Christmas we had a party, including the setting
> up of a crèche. I darkened the faces of Mary,
> Joseph, and Jesus to make the point in my sermon
> that Jesus was dark skinned and had a clearer iden-
> tification with black folks than with me. (The white
> lieutenant didn't like that at all.)[1]

While African-American theologians particularly helped us to see the racial and cultural aspects of Jesus' life and ministry, feminist theologians like Radford Ruether helped us to identify the feminine aspect of Jesus' character. One of the most tender images of Jesus is clearly feminine as he cries over Jerusalem and laments "Jerusalem, Jerusalem, the city that kills the prophets and stones those who are sent to it! How often have I desired to gather your children together as a hen gathers her brood under her wings, and you were not willing!" (Luke 13:34). Feminine images of Jesus and of God were rarely considered before women entered the theological discussion.

Feminist theologians helped the church realize that the images of women in Holy Scripture were culture-bound, incomplete, and insufficient. In this day and age I would hope that little would need to be said about how Paul's statement about women in I Corinthians 14:34-35 reflects a particular culture and time and cannot simply be imposed on women today. Yet over the centuries this and other similar passages of Scripture have been used as tools for the social-ization, if not subjugation, of women in private and public roles. But when women began to consider and interpret the biblical texts for themselves, different images and concerns emerged.

Professor Phyllis Byrd, one of the early Protestant women seminary professors in the US, wrote a brief essay on "onomastics" in the Old Testament. Onomastics deals with the study of proper names of men and women. In her essay, Byrd simply states that it is very telling that few female names in the Old Testament include "God" (El) as a part of the name, E̲lisheba (Elizabeth) being the most notable exception. On the other hand one can immediately surface many male names that include E̲l. Joe̲l, E̲lijah, E̲lisha, E̲liezer, and Danie̲l come to mind easily. In sharp contrast many of the names of the women are descriptive of certain characteristics of the woman and can even be derogatory. For example, one of the translations of Leah is "cow" and Rachel means "ewe" or lamb. The *el* of Rachel's name is not the same word in Hebrew for the name of God. So while men are identified through names that include God, women seem to be identified as mere cows and ewes! What implications might such an examination of common biblical names have on how we even today perceive the life and faith of women as compared to that of men? Byrd's essay is a simple but powerful statement about what can be learned by expanding the theological conversation.

Elisabeth Schüssler Fiorenza also challenged our perceptions of God through a new examination of Matthew 7:9-11 and Luke 11:11-13. The texts are similar and refer to the nature of God. Matthew and Luke have Jesus stating in slightly different ways that believers may approach God in prayer in the same way in which a child approaches a parent asking for food. In both texts the hearers are invited to look within themselves to their own experience as parents as they feed their children. If their child asked them for bread, fish, or an egg, would they give that child a stone or even worse a snake, or a scorpion instead? Of course not! Thus Jesus states that if those who are evil know how to respond in a caring way toward their children, then so much more can be expected of

God. All this is fine except that for nearly 2,000 years the church has assumed that the parent feeding the children is the father.

When Schüssler Fiorenza began to study these biblical texts anew she challenged the traditional interpretation by asserting that in patriarchal societies, such as those of first-century Palestine, it was the *mothers* who fed the children. Even in modern societies most children ask their mothers, not their fathers, for food. She concludes that Jesus was in fact suggesting that God is like a good mother who gives her children the best gifts, feeding their bodies and their spirits.

At another place in the theological dialogue, as liberation theologians unmasked the social location of past theological debates, it became apparent that in several controversies of the early church, power, rather than truth, had carried the day. One of the first theologians to resurrect an old heresy was Jürgen Moltmann in his book *The Crucified God.* The early church had declared that only the human part of Jesus had died on the cross and called this obvious heresy *Patripassianism.* Moltmann argued that the full incarnate Christ suffered the brutality of the cross; otherwise it separated God from all suffering humanity. Jesus Christ on the cross had not been vulnerable in part but rather had submitted fully to the vulnerability of suffering and even death. Moltmann's thinking was in line with that of liberation theologians who argued that because God in Christ had shared the vulnerability of the first-century occupied Palestine, Christ was also fully meaningful to vulnerable people in El Salvador, Somalia, and the ghettoes and barrios of America. How much richer is our understanding of what God has done for us through Jesus Christ because of the different voices of faith among us.

There are, however, even today, the voices of those who challenge any notions of knowing Jesus other than through very narrow ways. Orthodox Christians cry out for a return to orthodoxy. Their concern for standards by which to assure the promulgation of true faith is an important consideration. The issue of how we discern what is faithful to the gospel message is the ongoing theological task of the church—the whole church.

The Book of Discipline of The United Methodist Church—2004 defines theology as "our effort to reflect upon God's gracious action in our lives."[2] It further defines our theological task as:

- critical and constructive;
- individual and communal;
- contextual and incarnational.

Finally, *The Book of Discipline* states that our theological task is "essentially practical."[3] In every generation Christians must examine their faith for themselves. I cannot depend on the faith of my grandmother. I must be grounded in my own faith in order to address the life issues and concerns of my generation, a generation that has gained its own knowledge and awareness of the world we live in, and that must face its own challenges. We examine our faith in order to faithfully proclaim the good news of God's love for all the world.

Each one of us must answer Jesus' question, "But who do you say that I am?" (Matthew 16:15). Hopefully we answer this core question through much prayer, the disciplined study of Scripture, and reflection. But beyond our personal convictions to and about Jesus, the nature of who Jesus is unfolds in conversation with the community that forms the body of Jesus Christ, for faith in Jesus is about being called into discipleship with all who believe in him. Even then we are mindful of the fact that what we know about Jesus comes not from human intelligence, but rather through the gracious gift of God's Spirit who gives us understanding.

By God's own choice our theological task is incarnational for

God chooses to reveal God's self in human history through Jesus Christ. Nothing surpasses the eloquence of John in describing this reality:

> And the Word became flesh and lived among us,
> And we have seen his glory, the glory as of a father's
> only Son, full of grace and truth.
>
> (John 1:14)

And we believe that God, through the Holy Spirit, continues to be present and active in the world, reconciling the world to God and God's own purposes. Thus we too must be incarnationally involved in the world, participating with God in the transformation of the world. Ultimately, however, we measure the truth of our faith by its practical significance. Does it inform our daily decisions and actions? Does it help the church fulfill its mission and ministry? We strive not to simply articulate a theology, but rather we aspire to live by the promises and demands of the gospel of Jesus Christ.

Theologian John Cobb has dedicated much of his work in the last twenty years to the empowerment of laypersons in the church. He has stated that theology is too important to be left to the theologians; that is, to the professional theologians. All serious Christians need to engage in the focused and disciplined work of doing theology. This is not new, for the apostle Paul reminded the early believers that we would all be required to "be accountable to God" (Romans 14:12). It does take all of us under the guidance of the Holy Spirit to more clearly know Jesus.

Sadly, though, Christians sometimes take the position that only a particular understanding of faith, their understanding, is the absolute truth. Persons who disagree with them are viewed as betraying the Christian faith itself. *The United Methodist Hymnal* has a prayer that offers us a word of wisdom. The prayer comes from Kenya.

In Hymnal

> *From the cowardice that dares not face new truth,*
> *from the laziness that is contented with half-truth,*
> *from the arrogance that thinks it knows all truth,*
> *Good Lord, deliver me.*[4]

Saint Augustine once said that the three foundations of sin are fear, sloth, and pride. May God indeed deliver us from our sin!

Self-focused, narrow-minded theology leads to another danger; that of all too often demanding, blind obedience. Charles Kimball, in his book *When Religion Becomes Evil,* lists five warning signs that could potentially point to a religion becoming evil. Among the five signs Kimball lifts up are absolute truth claims and blind obedience. Jesus was in some ways creatively "disobedient" in relation to his childhood faith, Judaism, as was the apostle Paul. Jesus and Paul call us to be discerning rather than blindly obedient.

The late German theologian, Dorothee Sölle, wrote a short but powerful book that was translated into English as *Beyond Mere Obedience.* She grew up in Nazi Germany and remembered clearly how the number one virtue in that society was obedience, blind obedience. Sölle reminds us that blind obedience is contradictory to the liberating message of the Christ. We are not called to blindly obey words in the Bible or the church's creeds; rather we are summoned to wrestle with the spirit of those words, to dialogue with the voices of the past and to add our own voice to the chorus of the faithful. Jesus' interaction with his past was creative and dynamic, "you have heard...but I say..." (Matthew 5:21-48). If we follow the Risen One faithfully, we will not do it in blind obedience but in joyful response to the gift of God's grace that he represents.

Blind obedience undermines the faith and discipleship of the body of Jesus Christ for it leads the church to a stagnant place of thoughtlessness. Thoughtful, reflective, and prayerful consideration of our faith, and, more importantly, of where God is leading us and how we might be faithful to God, is critical to the life and mission of the church. Such consideration of faith and mission is not the work of the few, but of the many. Whose faith counts? The faith of each one of us.

4 Faith in Jesus in a Postmodern World

W hen my daughter Sofia was two years old she climbed on my desk as I was busy completing some work, moved my papers over so she could gain my undivided attention, and declared to me that she loved Jesus. It was to my mother's ears the sweetest confession of faith in Jesus Christ I had ever heard. I responded by taking her into my arms and telling her that I loved Jesus too, and that Jesus loved us both. The moment made me acutely aware of my responsibility to help this child of mine grow and live her faith in Jesus. It has not been an easy task.

My daughter's faith questions over the years have often made me defensive as I have attempted to prove faith to her. Her questions have provided the opportunity to test on her my ability to rationally explain the many issues that have arisen throughout the history of Christianity. At the age of four, in the middle of a busy grocery store aisle, she once asked her father, "Papa, why did they crucify Jesus?" He readily responded that her question was best left to her mother, the preacher. How do you explain to a child of four the horror of human sin at its worst?

In some ways there is nothing more difficult than explaining faith to a child. It isn't that their minds aren't able to comprehend the answers, but rather that most adults have a need to provide concrete answers. I realized that the more faith questions my daughter had the more defensive I became because I could not always give her concrete answers. The fact that at two years of age my daughter had been satisfied to hear that I, like her, loved Jesus should have been a lesson to me, but I wanted to do more than simply say that I loved Jesus and believed in him.

What became clear to me in this process of living with my child's evolving faith was that I had been shaped by a modern worldview that depends on scientific proof to explain all things. The skepticism and the rationalism of the Enlightenment continue to have their influence on society and even on me, a person of Christian faith.

I am a child of the "Is God dead?" era, an era that declared that science had won over faith and that those matters that could not be substantiated by scientific method were simply unreal. The Bible and faith, however, cannot be explained along the lines of the scientific proof expected by modernity. How can we possibly explain the sustaining grace of manna in the wilderness for the Hebrews escaping slavery, or the miracles of healing in Scripture, or the resurrection of Jesus? It is by faith alone that we understand Scripture and believe these things and understand their significance for our lives.

I am reminded of the anguished father of Mark 9:14-27. His son was possessed by a spirit that left him unable to speak. When the spirit would seize him, it would dash him down, make him foam at the mouth, grind his teeth, and become rigid. Sometimes the harmful spirit would throw the boy into the fire or into the water, almost destroying him. The father had already asked Jesus' disciples to heal his son, but they had been unable to do so. After chastising the disciples for their lack of faith, Jesus called upon the father to bring the boy to him.

With trepidation and doubt the father brought the boy before

Jesus, openly demonstrating his lack of faith as he said to Jesus, "...*if* you are able to do anything, have pity on us and help us" (Mark 9:22c). Jesus was clearly perturbed by the father and appeared to shout back at him, "If you are able!—All things can be done for the one who believes" (Mark 9:23). Scripture tells us that, "Immediately the father of the boy cried out, 'I believe; help my unbelief!'" (Mark 9:24).

The story reminds us that in matters of faith believing is more important than understanding, and prayer is critical to our faith. Befuddled by their inability to free the boy of the harmful spirit, the disciples asked Jesus in private why they could not cast it out. Jesus' reply was that this kind of spirit could be driven out only through prayer (Mark 9:28-29). We would do well to constantly ask Jesus through prayer to help our unbelief.

Fortunately, postmodernism no longer solely depends on the rigid measures of scientific proof. Out of learned necessity, postmodernism leaves room for mystery and the often complex and sometimes even unknown dimensions of truth. Our postmodern world provides us with opportunities to bring a word of hope to a world that, in spite of all of humankind's achievements and advancements, cannot fill the deep yearnings of the heart. The apostle Paul still stands today as the greatest Christian evangelist precisely because he understood that the gospel of Christ Jesus with all its mystery filled the deep yearnings of the human heart.

The earliest Christology found in Scripture is not found in the New Testament Gospels as one might expect but rather in Paul's writings. Writing as early as 50 C.E., and thus before the authors of the Gospels, Paul writes from a very personal core of belief as he relates his encounter with the Risen Christ. His statements are more theological than historical narrative; that is, he says little about the earthly ministry of Jesus Christ, choosing instead to focus on how Christ can be present in the lives of those who

believe. I take comfort in the fact that Paul arrived at a very profound, personal, and passionate faith in, and relationship with,
Jesus Christ without the benefit of the Gospel narratives. If it is
possible for Paul to believe in Jesus without knowing many of the
details we receive from the Gospel writers Matthew, Mark, Luke,
and John, we also can be persons of Christian faith even without
all the details present in the Gospels.

Paul does not need to demonstrate his belief in the Risen One
with a long, detailed story. Rather he gives witness to what he saw,
how Jesus appeared to him. The statement in I Corinthians 15:1-
7 is probably the earliest written story of the post-Resurrection
appearances of Jesus. In this passage Paul states simply that:

> Christ died for our sins in accordance with the scrip-
> tures, and that he was buried, and that he was raised
> on the third day, in accordance with the scriptures,
> and that he appeared to Cephas, then to the twelve.
> Then he appeared to more than five hundred broth-
> ers and sisters at one time...Then he appeared to
> James, and then to all the apostles.
>
> (I Corinthians 15:3-7)

Paul then gives witness to the Lord having also appeared to him.
It is in having the Lord visit him as he did that Paul can claim to also
be an apostle of Christ Jesus, thereby demonstrating his apostolic
credentials, even if he is self-effacing as he states that he is "one
untimely born" (I Corinthians 15:8).

As an aside it is interesting that I Corinthians 15 fails to
mention Jesus' appearance to Mary Magdalene which suggests
that the struggle between those who supported the women's
witness of the resurrection of Jesus and those who supported
the emerging patriarchal hierarchy within the community of

Christian faith was already occurring by the time Paul became a convert. Only Cephas and James are singled out as individuals to whom Jesus had appeared, the very leaders with whom Paul had conferred as we know from the letter to the Galatians (Galatians 1:18-19), and also the leaders of the faction that did not want Gentiles to be included in the new Christian movement.

Even a thorough study of the Gospels does not give us sufficient information about Jesus to be able to historically and scientifically prove his existence, that he was the Incarnation of God among us, or that he was resurrected from death. We believe in Jesus not because we have historical and scientific proof but because of faith alone. Ephesians states that by grace we have been saved, through faith; something we cannot do for ourselves, but that comes as a gift of God (Ephesians 2:8).

The spirit of Ephesians 2:8 helps us avoid unnecessary controversies about details that some might find difficult, if not impossible, to believe. An elderly pastor when asked if he believed in the virgin birth answered, "I stand with Paul on that issue." Paul's statements on the birth of Jesus are not in narrative form but in passionate and poetic statements such as the lovely birth announcement found in Galatians—"But when the fullness of time had come, God sent his Son, born of a woman, born under the law," (Galatians 4:4). Or the hymn about Christian character found in Philippians:

> Let the same mind be in you that was in Christ
> Jesus, who, though he was in the form of God,
> did not regard equality with God as something to
> be exploited, but emptied himself, taking the
> form of a slave, being born in human likeness."
>
> (Philippians 2:5-7a)

The smart, elderly pastor who stood with Paul on the "how" of the Incarnation was aligning himself with a most valid, biblically grounded Christology, the Christology of Paul. The real "scandal" of the Christian faith is that we dare to affirm that God was in Christ, that the Word became flesh; real flesh, vulnerable flesh! This is the common affirmation of all the Christologies found in the New Testament even if they vary in the details of how they help us to see the Incarnation.

Mark, in all probability the earliest Gospel writer, shows us God incarnated in Jesus through Jesus' baptism:

> And just as he was coming up out of the water, he saw the heavens torn apart and the Spirit descending like a dove on him. And a voice came from heaven, "You are my Son, the Beloved; with you I am well pleased."
>
> (Mark 1:10-11)

In his short Gospel, Mark gives us another glimpse of Jesus as the Incarnation of God among us when the centurion at the cross sees Jesus breathe his last breath on the cross and proclaims, "Truly this man was God's Son!" (Mark 15:39). Mark, interestingly enough, does not provide details about the Resurrection, he merely gives us an empty tomb and astonished women. That may not be good enough for many, but it was good enough for Mark and for Paul. They believed even without the details! I can live with differences in details, seeking instead agreement on that which is fundamentally crucial; believing that Christ, the Son of God, became flesh, revealed God's heart and will to us, that he suffered, died on a cross, and lives again.

Paul, Mark, and John all believe in the Incarnation but they don't give us narratives for how that Incarnation happened. Matthew and Luke only say that the Incarnation occurred by action of the Holy Spirit. Mark and Paul believe in the resurrection of Jesus but again do not offer any narrative about how the Resurrection occurred. Matthew, Luke, and John include resurrection narratives of an empty grave, of angels explaining the absence of Jesus' body in the tomb, and even of Jesus appearing to Mary, but none explain how the resurrection of Jesus came to be. The Gospel writers and Paul all believe in the Incarnation and the Resurrection and all of us who call ourselves Christians must affirm these two claims of our faith, whether or not we assert or affirm every detail of the specific narratives offered in Scripture. What is core to our Christian faith is that Jesus Christ is both the incarnate Word and the resurrected Lord.

I mentioned earlier that the Gospel of Mark ends with a disturbing "empty grave" story with astonished and fearful women (Mark 16:8). This Gospel ending concerned the early church and a longer ending was added relatively early on (Mark 16:9-20). The Revised Standard Version and the New Revised Standard Version of the Bible take note of this addition, the King James Version does not. The longer ending is a mélange of statements taken from the other Gospels and from other traditions. It is not necessary to point out all the details. For the purposes of this book it is enough to simply point out that the Gospel of Mark originally ended with an "empty grave" resurrection story. This does not mean that Mark did not believe in the Resurrection, quite the opposite. Mark seemed to have no need to "prove" the Resurrection with a detailed story. For Mark, faith in our resurrected Lord was truth sufficient for the journey of Christian faith.

Postmodernity, however, does not simply seek a measurement of proof, even with space for mystery. Postmodernity argues for the possibility of many approaches to truth. The French philosopher

Jean-Francois Lyotard defines postmodernism as the rejection of all meta-narratives. By "meta-narratives" he refers to universal worldviews, discourses, and definitions which have been constructed by dominant power arrangements. He states that we each have different stories, our individual narratives, to tell from different perspectives, embodied in our religions, our myths, our cultural legends, but none of them carries the absolute truth about the nature of things. According to Lyotard, there can be no one true story, no grand theory that informs us of the meaning of life, and hence no account of absolute good and evil, right or wrong, that is true for all persons. This is the basic argument of Lyotard in his book *The Postmodern Condition: A Report on Knowledge.* How did we arrive at this postmodern condition? Lyotard explains the postmodern condition by stating that all knowing and understanding involve interpretation in terms of a point of view, and human points of view are local and particular to the person or community seeking to know or to understand such things as God, life, faith, and how we are to live with God and with each other. Because of this it is impossible to find one universal story that explains God, life, faith, and how we are to live with God and with each other, that makes sense to all of us; a story that stands above all people and communities, our histories and our cultures, making sense to all of us.

Modernism, the age previous to the postmodern one, was supposed to figure this out, but failed. We were, in fact, doomed to fail, according to Lyotard, because even our human reason, our ways of thinking, are conditioned by the languages we speak and the traditions that we have. What seems objective reasoning, objective subjecthood, "rational" or "reasonable" from one perspective will not seem so from another.[1]

It is argued that postmodernist views, like Lyotard's, have dangerous implications for ethics and politics, because they allow no absolute or universal claims about right and wrong. But postmodernists characteristically respond that absolutist claims are the real danger in ethics and politics, because those who claim to have the absolute right usually look down upon or marginalize those persons or groups whose views or behavior do not fit their norms. It's quite a conundrum!

Consider, however, the fact that within the New Testament we have several Christologies, each one of which could be seen as absolute. The wisdom of those who established the canon, the books approved for inclusion in the New Testament, leads us well. That wisdom is seen in the inclusion of four Gospels even with their differences, rather than choosing only one. Marcion, as noted earlier, preferred only one Gospel, Mark, but that was found to be a troublesome "absolute claim." The people who fixed the canon were aware of the inconsistencies and discrepancies in the Gospels but they committed themselves to radical inclusivity because it provided a clearer reflection, a more complete picture, of the teachings of Jesus Christ.

Perhaps one of the most difficult texts for preachers to share with their congregations is the final judgment of Matthew 25. This passage makes church attendance, creedal statements, pledges, offerings, benevolences, even church affiliation, totally irrelevant or unnecessary. The only thing that seems to matter according to this passage is our doing, not our talking. Entrance into the bliss of the reward of the King is granted only to those who acted as mercifully as Jesus acted during his earthly ministry. This is a parallel of the Old Testament prophetic admonition that God is pleased not with pious liturgies but with merciful deeds (Micah 6:6-8, Isaiah 1:10-17, Jeremiah 9:23-24).

Here again it would be against either Jesus' character or the wisdom of those who created the canon to say this is all that is really needed. That would turn the "doing" into another "absolute claim." What we are all called to do is to live in the dynamic tension of competing claims within the Gospels and within the entire Bible.

In doing so we will be better equipped to live in a pluralistic world allowing room for the competing claims of Judaism, Islam, Buddhism, Hinduism, and other faith expressions. Even then, what is particularly dangerous about our time is that conservative elements within each of the Abrahamic faiths, Judaism, Islam, and Christianity, are vociferously making "absolute truth claims," thereby hardening each other's stances and endangering major regions of the world. This should be a grave concern for us, as Christians and as citizens of the world, impacting our discipleship in the world.

Discipleship in the name of Jesus Christ is at the heart of our faith. We believe with James that faith without works is dead. John Wesley, the founder of Methodism, organized the early Methodists around the practice of faith. According to Wesley personal holiness is inextricably linked to social holiness. True spirituality always expresses itself in love of God, neighbor, and even enemy. Wesley believed and practiced a faith that, while holding firm to the core beliefs of Christian faith, allowed for theological differences of a more minor dimension. In the midst of a theological controversy he once stated to one who held a different opinion on a matter of Christian faith, "If your heart is like mine, then give me your hand, and brothers we shall be."

Methodism has never been creedal in nature. Rather, we seek the table of Christian conferencing where in our diversity we hold each other accountable in Christian love, teach and practice the means of grace, and support and encourage each other to be faithful to the one we claim as Lord and Savior, namely, Jesus the Christ. Jesus is the name above all names; the salvation of the world. Intentional efforts to come to know the experience of God of persons from other living faiths of the world, however, affirm for us that God's mercy is beyond our understanding. The witness of Jesus as he loved all persons, must be the model of our discipleship.

As more and more voices participate in the theological dialogue, the possibilities of solving our most difficult and divisive issues will increase. Imagine what kind of a church we would be if the institutional decisions we make emerged from an incarnational theological stance rather than from clever parliamentary procedures. Living out an incarnational theology will require that we be willing to be in dialogue across the church and even across faith lines. Dialogue implies openness and vulnerability, on the one hand, and respect for the dignity of the persons with whom we are establishing dialogue, on the other. People often overlook the meaning of the word dialogue and fail to honor the process the word implies.

Dialogue comes from two Greek terms we should be acquainted with, especially as Christians. Logue comes from *logos*, word; the very term used by the writer of the Gospel of John to refer to the event of the Incarnation, the logos becoming flesh (John 1:1-4). The Word which became flesh lives a perfect relationship between word and deed. We as Christians may from time to time close the gap between our words and deeds through the grace of the One whose word and deeds were one. The *dia* portion of dialogue means through, as in diameter, so that dialogue means that activity in which the words of others enter our being, and go through our defenses and our fears. Active listening is a term used by counselors helping people to communicate. Active listening means letting the other person's words come into our very being, allowing the logos to indeed penetrate our defenses.

Now, more than ever, we face a time in much need of honest and open theological dialogue. The participation of many voices, educated voices, sensitive voices, theological voices, biblically-grounded voices, voices from the intersection of human life and the encounter of the Holy One, will overcome the human tendencies toward separation, isolation, and hierarchical and authoritarian power over others, in church and in society.

A theology that is based on prayerful dialogue, that is critical and constructive, individual and communal, contextual and incarnational, and that trusts Holy Scripture as it invokes the wisdom of the Holy Spirit, can provide a needed corrective to those who believe that only one way, their way, is the correct one. Truth that emerges from the dialogue that is carried out in the midst of differences honestly confronted is more acceptable and believable over the long haul than "truth" that is imposed from a position of power. The history of the church is replete with examples where a small faction claiming to have "the truth" persecuted and destroyed those who disagreed. Roman Catholics usually take a hard hit because of the Inquisition, but plenty of examples abound of Protestant intolerance and cruelty. Geneva under Calvinist theocrats was every bit as bad in principle as Spain and the inquisitors. As we lift up our voices and proclaim our faith in Jesus Christ we need to learn from his own humility and allow the religious claims of other faiths to exist side by side with us. This is very difficult to do unless we commit ourselves to the dialogue I mention above. If we are to survive as a nation of immigrants and in a world of differences we need to understand our faith claims as well as the faith claims of others.

I believe in Jesus and I believe that he is for me the "way, truth, and life." I am called to share that faith with passion and conviction with those around me, but I should not make claims that diminish the integrity and dignity of those who sincerely practice a religion other than Christianity. I am fully aware of the Great Commission found in Matthew 28:18-20 and the responsibility of every Christian to fulfill Jesus' command, but I need to see others within the framework of love of neighbor and even enemy that

Jesus gave to his disciples. I must also see it within the understanding that the Holy Spirit alone convinces the heart in matters of faith. While the Holy Spirit may use my witness to touch the heart of another, faith is always dependent on the action of the Holy Spirit within our hearts.

5 Envisioning a Faithful Church in a Postmodern World

I n the church we tend to respond to the postmodern age in two ways. On the one hand, we throw our hands up in the air in despair and state that the church is doomed for people no longer believe in God, and no longer seem to have any need of or interest in the church and its ministry. On the other hand, we seem oblivious to what century we are living in. I want to suggest that living in the postmodern age should not bring us despair, nor should we ignore its realities, for to live in the postmodern age is to find incredible opportunities to share the love of God, and isn't that what we are called to do as people of Christian faith?

The *New York Times Magazine* of January 29, 2006, had an intriguing article called "The Post-Colonial Missionary—What in God's Name Evangelicals Are Doing in Africa" by Daniel Bergner. In the article we learn of the Maples family from suburban California who have gone to Kurungu in northern Kenya to work with the Samburu people. It is quite a change for the Maples. They had moved from an enormous California home to a hut of a house on the continent of Africa, from a family dog to baboons that move about feeding on tiny buds outside their home, from speaking English to struggling to learn a language that their ear has difficulty hearing. Their nine- and twelve-year-old daughters had to make new friends. Meghan, the twelve-year-old, was invited to the celebration of a Samburu girl her age. She was honored to be invited. What she experienced at the celebration will stay with her the rest of her life. On the night of the celebration she wrote in her diary, "I saw something I don't think I will ever forget. I saw a girl get mutilated. A thirteen-year-old girl having something awful done." The awful thing that Meghan had seen was the female circumcision of this Samburu girl. Why would the Maples go to such a place?

The Maples say they have gone to Kurungu, Kenya, in response to humanity's dire need; a need that is both spiritual and earthly. What have they learned? They share that they have learned that God doesn't speak one language, and that Christian worship must take indigenous forms. Though we have often ignored this learning, I believe Christians have known this for a long, long time. At the same time, cultural practices such as female circumcision need to be addressed with the help of women's rights groups in the respective cultures. The relationship between gospel and culture is an ongoing, contextual issue.

I remember as a young college student being given the great opportunity to serve as a director of the General Board of Global Ministries of The United Methodist Church. To see how The United Methodist Church, alongside ecumenical and community partners, was serving throughout the world was an amazing experience that would shape my faith and my ministry. I learned how, from its inception, the Methodist movement on the North American continent has been active in mission to the world around it. The historic mission agencies of the church have led our denomination's evolving ministry in the world with courage and passion.

By the early 1970s, however, the work of the General Board of Global Ministries was under attack for doing missionary work that recognized that, even before we ever arrived at a place in the world, God was already there; that the great diversity of the world's cultures, languages, and sensibilities were not an error but part of God's great master plan in creation; and that persons in other parts of the world were not any less intelligent, wise, creative, spiritually alert, and sensitive than we were, they were just different and we had much to learn from them. We have known what the Maples have learned in their recent venture out into the world, known it for a long time, so why then the criticism of the General Board of Global Ministries?

No denominational agency has ever been without its institutional weaknesses or failures, but after living in this church as long as I have, I believe the criticism that began to chisel away at this mission agency and eventually at the denomination itself was a reflection of a church assuming the secular arrogance of a nation that had grown to believe that it was the epitome of human perfection. That God's favor was with the US in a way and that God did not extend divine favor and presence to the rest of the world became an embedded aspect of this corrupt view of the church and its mission. The world needed to be saved from itself and only good news from US soil, with all its wrappings and trappings, could bring salvation.

In the latter part of the last century, interestingly enough, the world came to reside in the US. At the beginning of this third millennium the US is racially and culturally as diverse as the world. Muslims, Buddhists, and Hindus, in growing numbers, live side by side with Christians in this country that once prided itself on being a predominantly Anglo-Saxon and Christian nation. Many Christian communities have attempted to faithfully give witness to Jesus Christ in the midst of such diversity. As a result, some

Christian congregations have changed from white to multicultural, from traditional to contemporary, in their worship and in their way of being the church. Some congregations have strived to be fully inclusive of all God's children including the poor, the outcast, and the rejected. Movements within the church have also challenged the church's exclusionary institutional policies that have maintained gay, lesbian, bisexual, and transgender persons on the edges of the church solely because of their sexual orientation. Interfaith dialogue has strengthened communities afflicted by discrimination and a lack of mutual understanding across cultural and religious differences.

Acknowledgment of differences and narratives from various social locations is a key condition of postmodernism. Let me share an experience from my context. In September of 2004, I began to serve as a bishop of The United Methodist Church. I have received no greater honor and no greater privilege in my life than that of being called forth and set apart for the ministry of general oversight and supervision of the church. The love I have carried in my heart for the church throughout my life only further deepens each day as I serve as a bishop of the church. I yearn to faithfully lead the church in its primary task of making disciples of Jesus Christ for the transformation of the world. I strive to direct my days in a manner that enables me to work to equip God's people for service in the church and in the world in the name of Jesus Christ, supporting and encouraging the ministry of all Christians. As a bishop I understand this privileged task to be done in the context of life itself. When I arrived at my assigned area to begin my work as an episcopal leader of the church I quickly encountered life itself.

On September 1, 2004, I picked up the local newspaper and read about a proposition that was before the legislature of one of the states in our area. The focus of the proposition was that of curbing illegal immigration. Though immigration is a federal matter, some in the state legislature were taking it upon themselves to fix the immigration problem through the denial of basic human services not only to undocumented immigrants but even to their US-born children. The tenor of the conversation around this proposition was heated and very racist. After carefully reading the proposition I found it both unhelpful and dangerous, politically and socially. Even more, I found it contrary to our Christian understanding of how we are to treat the sojourner, the immigrant, the stranger among us. I chose to take my very first public stand on this matter remembering that bishops of The United Methodist Church are to be prophetic voices and courageous leaders in the cause of justice for all people.

The first response I received to what I wrote about this immigration proposition was the following short message:

> "I respectfully suggest that the Bishop confine her epistles to matters of the Church and stay out of politics."

This person's response did not surprise me. I have heard things like this all of my ministry. When I read the respondent's words, the first thought that went through my mind was, "What Bible is this person reading for it is not the Bible I am reading!" The person suggested that I confine my work to matters of the church. I thought to myself, now what would Jesus define as matters of the church? Jesus took on the political empires of his time by holding up the alternative vision of communities of justice and peace where every single person is important; communities where the orphan, the widow, the sojourner, the poor, the outcast, are cared for in special ways. Jesus proclaimed that the reign of God had arrived; a reign that brings about a new social and personal reality even in the midst of this life. Jesus, our Risen Lord, whose very Resurrection proclaims that "God has made him both Lord and Messiah" (Acts 2:36), above all, Jesus the One whom we profess as Savior. So what are matters of the church? According to the witness of Holy Scripture, all of life falls under the care and concern of Christ Jesus, and thus, as Christ's disciples, all of life with its personal and social, its political, socioeconomic, and cultural dimensions falls under the concern of the church for we are the church of Christ Jesus. Jesus passionately cares about all of life, and about each one of us.

Marcus Borg, in his book *The Heart of Christianity: Rediscovering a Life of Faith*, speaks to the political nature of the biblical message. He says:

> If we ask why the God of the Bible cares about politics, about systemic justice, the answer is disarmingly simple. God cares about justice because the God of the Bible cares about suffering. And the single biggest cause of unnecessary human suffering throughout history has been and is unjust social systems.[1]

I continue to attempt to give a faithful witness to God whose care challenges every social system that brings human suffering. As I dealt more and more with the issue of immigration, however, it became clear to me that many of the negative and even hostile responses I was hearing to my episcopal pleas that we care for the immigrants as Scripture calls us to care for them, were coming from places of fear. Persons feared losing their jobs and communities and even their churches to immigrants they did not know and were suspicious of. One day, while praying, it occurred to me that we had to create opportunities for conversation among us about this important concern.

I remembered our commitment as United Methodists to Christian conferencing.

John Wesley spoke of Christian conferencing as a means of grace. God's people gather for conversation, seeking to discern God's will on that which is before them. Bishop Kenneth Carder illuminates our Wesleyan understanding of Christian conferencing in a most helpful way. He states:

> • The conversation is formed and shaped by grace, which is the presence and power of God. Responding to and expressing God's grace is the motive, not winning an argument or advancing an agenda. The manner and spirit in which decisions are made has priority over the tally of the votes in authentic Christian conferencing.
>
> • The conversation is purposeful and edifying. Being a channel of grace to the hearers and building up the community is the goal.
>
> • Christian conversation begins, continues, and ends in prayer. Indeed it is a form of prayer!"[2]

I invited the clergy and lay members of my area to gather for Christian conferencing on the issue of immigration. Three settings for Christian conferencing were identified and the invitation was extended. Persons from every political perspective came. It took a bit of explanation about what Christian conferencing meant and how it was done, but soon we were into deep and heartfelt conversation. By the end of the Christian conferencing the mood in our area had shifted from anger and frustration on all sides to one of prayerful consideration of a matter that affects all of us.

Along the way the Council of Bishops asked me if I would be their spokesperson at a national rally on immigration that was being held in Washington, DC. I accepted the request with fear and trepidation. I was honored and humbled by the invitation. As the day of the national rally approached I realized more and more what a tremendous responsibility I had assumed. I worried about what I should say, how I should say it, and whether I could ever say it effectively. I finally decided that I simply needed to focus on God and bringing a word from God for God's people.

When I arrived at the National Mall in Washington, DC, on that April afternoon I was taken aback by the crowd. Estimates were that there were half a million people there. The people just kept coming up until the last hour. There were Hispanics/Latinos from every Latin American country but there were also Haitians and Africans, people from the Philippines and from China, Russians and Bulgarians, Czechoslovakians and Hungarians. They were a tapestry of the diversity of all God's children. It took my breath away to see all these people; people hungry for a word of justice, a word of hope, and a word of life.

When it came my turn to speak, this great multitude had already heard a dozen speakers, from Senator Ted Kennedy to community organizers working in the trenches. I was ready to have my small part done. When my turn came I stood before those hundreds of thousands of people and I said three simple things. "I stand before you this day as a bishop of The United Methodist Church," I said to the great crowd. "And as the daughter of immigrants," I shared. Then I said the word that they were yearning to hear. I said, "I come before you to tell you that God is with you." At that very moment the crowd went wild, drowning me out with a roar of thunderous applause and shouts of joy. I tried to say a few more things but it was impossible for me to be heard for they had heard what their hearts needed; God was with them, with us. It is true that every time we proclaim the true word that God is with us, God's people will experience the glory and the power, the love and the grace of God come shining through, giving hope and life itself.

At the end of that day I returned to my area having seen in those gathered at the National Mall the human face of the issue of immigration. I was grateful to God that I was returning to an area that was prayerfully attempting to discern God's will on this issue. I had barely arrived back at my office when the nasty calls began, however. What struck me most was that the persons calling all had the same question for me. What gave me the right to speak for The United Methodist Church, they asked. I found myself quickly and somewhat naively sharing that I had gone at the request of the Council of Bishops of our church. But even after giving this response the negative callers would ask me the question again. What gave me the right to speak for The United Methodist Church?

In the days and weeks to follow, my efforts to respond to these persons who were not only challengers of my very presence at this immigration rally, but also members of congregations under my care, were of no avail. I found these brothers and sisters resistant to any semblance of Christian conferencing. In some cases civil conversation was even difficult.

Subsequently, a publication of the Institute on Religion and Democracy (IRD) targeted at United Methodists would criticize my participation and the very brief statement I had made at the national rally on immigration. The article ended by asking United Methodists to contact me and ask me the question, "What gave me the right to speak for The United Methodist Church?"[3]

In The United Methodist Church only the General Conference can speak on behalf of the church. It is a right granted exclusively to the General Conference under our Constitution.

Yet I do believe that bishops are called to proclaim God's justice as contained in Scripture, and to speak boldly and unequivocally that which we United Methodists have together discerned through Christian conferencing to be God's will for our lives and for the world. As United Methodists we have clear Christian teachings on the issue of immigration and the Council of Bishops had asked me to publicly articulate our teachings.

As Christians in the US we have become fearful; fearful of the world, overwhelmed by its vastness, its complexity, and its enormous challenges. We have become overwhelmed by the world to the point of anger, an anger that pushes us to want to control and dominate it out of the fear that it will consume and destroy us. In the anger I suspect is the greater unspoken and perhaps unconscious fear that the love of God cannot possibly be sufficient for all the world.

When I was a child, I loved to imagine the world from my small bed by the window in the bedroom I shared with one of my sisters. My world at that time was our extended family's farm populated by my grandparents, aunts and uncles, cousins, and my immediate family. That was my world. It was a world stretched only by an occasional visit to town and our active participation in our Methodist church. My world was a small world but I loved to imagine the rest of the world. So as I lay on my small bed by the window I would look out into the darkness of night, sometimes illuminated by the moon and the stars, and I would imagine the great expanse of God's world.

It was like high-speed travel seen through my mind's eye. When the television series *Star Trek* was introduced I had no problem believing that Scotty, the spaceship engineer, could beam people to another place in time and space for I could see it. High-speed travel around the world was possible. And so, in my mind's eye in the deep of night, I would travel around the world seeing towns and cities, open fields and busy roads, mountains, lakes, and seas with floating icebergs, islands, peninsulas, and whole continents, birds and wild beasts, dogs and cats, and water creatures I'd never imagined before. And I would see people; people who looked like me and spoke my language, and people of different hues and cultures, whose tongues resounded in tones unfamiliar to my ear. Pretty soon excitement would turn to weariness and weariness to fear as I contemplated the world and its peoples. What would start as an exercise of discovery through the imagination would leave me feeling overwhelmed, for the world was too big, too complex, too busy, too confusing for my child's mind. So I would push the world out of my mind in order to be able to sleep.

One day, though, I heard a verse of Scripture that made me look at the world differently. Even as a child I am sure that I had heard this verse before, but on that day it spoke to me in a way that brought me comfort. It was the verse that captures the heart and essence of that which we proclaim as good news. It was John 3:16. You know this verse:

> For God so loved the world that he gave his only
> Son, so that everyone who believes in him may not
> perish but may have eternal life.

"For God so loved the world"—suddenly the world ceased to be an overwhelming and frightening place for I could see the world, all of the world, valleys and mountains, rivers and seas, lush fields and barren deserts, earth and sky, and every living creature, being held in God's own arms; tender loving arms, the arms of our loving creator holding us like a loving father, a loving mother. For God loves the world. My childhood fear subsided as I realized that the world was in God's care. It was a sacred moment; a gift of the Holy Spirit.

I wonder if this was the kind of experience John Wesley had on May 24, 1738, at the gathering of Christians on Aldersgate Street, when his heart was strangely warmed as he heard Martin Luther's preface to the Letter of Paul to the Romans and felt that God's mercy extended even to him. He knew by the touch of the Holy Spirit that he was in God's care. Faith is not so much about what we do, but rather about what God has decided to do for us as God gifts us with divine mercy and grace, doing for us what we cannot do for ourselves. By grace we are saved by faith (Romans 5:1-2, Ephesians 2:4-9).

I am so glad that the Holy Spirit never ceases its work in our lives. Instead it continues to bring us sacred moments, divine gifts of grace. A few years later I heard this same holy word once again. It was at my confirmation. My pastor stood before us and invited us to profess our faith with the words of John 3:16, and then looking at all of us and each of us, he said, "This is the God whom you will serve—God who loves the world." He was very clear. That God loves the world did not mean that anything goes, but it did mean that the way God had chosen to reach out to the world was through love; a love so profound that God was willing to allow Christ his Son to die on a cross for you and me and all the world. A love so profound that from that cruel cross Jesus would raise his voice and beg for our salvation—"Father, forgive them for they do not know what they are doing" (Luke 23:34). I look across the church and I wonder if Jesus might be saying those same words today. "Father, forgive them for they do not know what they are doing," as we judge each other, fight with each other, exclude each other, and sometimes even crucify each other.

We dare to judge, to fight, exclude, and some days even crucify each other, and we do it in the name of Jesus who came that we might know the love of God! The world looks upon us, incredulous, unbelieving, remaining untransformed. Can we blame the world? I keep before me, though, the hope that we can be, by the grace of God, the embodiment of the grace and love of God, leaving behind judgment, fighting, exclusion, and our need to destroy others. What has become abundantly clear to me is that becoming the embodiment of the grace and love of God is going to take having a faith that enables us to line up behind Jesus; not behind our political persuasions, not behind our pet projects, not behind our protected pockets or our petty power struggles, but behind Jesus.

One summer day not that long ago, I took a walk in the desert. I was not alone. Traveling down to the border between Arizona and Sonora, Mexico, 150 Christians walked in the desert in order to learn more about what was being described as the immigration crisis of the US. As the United Methodist bishop of the area I sent out the notice of the walk to our congregations and United Methodists lined up. The Democrats lined up to the left and the Republicans lined up to the right! I kept waiting for good United Methodists to line up behind Jesus, Son of God, the God who says to us to treat the immigrant, the sojourner among us, as a native-born, as one of us, loving them as we love ourselves, for we were once sojourners in the land of captivity (Leviticus 19:33-34). Having a faith that enables us to line up behind Jesus always requires that radical action of receiving others with the fullness of love. It is not always easy, but always necessary if we are to be disciples of Jesus Christ.

When I was first assigned to the area where I serve as an episcopal leader, I decided that in my first year of service in the area I would visit every single congregation and ministry institution in my area. The experience was very moving as I saw God's people living out their faith throughout a vast region of the country. Every once in a while there would be, however, a congregation that saddened me, not because of their size, or the shape of their buildings, or their economic condition, but because of the state of their soul.

One afternoon out visiting the churches in a particular district I noticed that the district superintendent appeared to be nervous. I turned and asked him if there was something bothering him. He turned to me and with a measure of concern in his eyes he said to me, "Bishop, I'm afraid you're going to be disappointed at this next church." I remember saying to him, "If there are five persons at the next church who love and serve the Lord and their neighbor, I will be pleased."

We arrived at a tiny little church in an obviously poor community and, lo and behold, there were exactly five church members there to welcome us! After a moment of introductions we sat in an informal circle and I invited the church members to share with me about their ministry. I kept listening for signs of love of God and love of and service to neighbor. When, after about twenty minutes, I had heard no clear signs of a congregation living the Great Commandment, I decided that they simply needed a bit of help in expressing themselves, so I asked them a question to help them out. "Tell me about your community," I said. It was a simple enough question, but one that triggered a most unexpected response.

A man seated directly across from me in the circle leaned forward toward me and with a scornful look upon his face he said to me, "This community is full of rotten people, and we don't need a single one of them in our church!" As soon as the words were out of his mouth, the other four church members all shook their heads in agreement. I had done my homework before visiting this church and knew that they were part of a community that was struggling with growing poverty. I also knew that in the global shift of populations they had recently become a predominantly Hispanic community. The church members weren't necessarily mean-spirited people. They were fearful people, afraid for their lives and afraid of those around them. They had forgotten that they and all in their community are in God's care, within the embrace of God's loving and tender arms.

As I write this book, the Judicial Council of The United Methodist Church has just declared that a pastor can exclude persons from membership in the church if they are not heterosexual. The specific case on which the Council ruled is one where a gay man of Christian faith asked to become a member of a United Methodist church in which he had become an active participant. The pastor denied him membership because he is a homosexual man, even though he professes and practices Christian faith. The love of God excludes no one, not even sinners like me and you. Loving others in their difference from us can be frightening, but we should not allow fear to enslave us.

In faith we are called to truly believe that God liberates us to love in ways that we did not imagine possible. Through the love of God we shall be truly free to love, truly liberated to serve one another in love. Paul wrote about this love as a mark of the community of the Spirit when in Galatians 5:1, 13-14, he states:

> For freedom Christ has set us free. Stand firm, therefore, and do not submit again to a yoke of slavery...For you were called to freedom, brothers and sisters; only do not use your freedom as an opportunity for self-indulgence, but through love become slaves to one another. For the whole law is summed up in a single commandment, "You shall love your neighbor as yourself."

Our faith leads us to share God's love and to share it unconditionally as we have been loved by God. Christian love, however, is not a love reserved only for those who are or may become

Christians. The love of Christ Jesus compels us to love all God's children. Phil Wogaman tells a great story in his book, *To Serve the Present Age: The Gift and Promise of United Methodism*, that makes this point in a deeply moving way.

One night he was at a hospital in Washington, DC, visiting one of the members of his congregation and offering prayer. Afterward, long after visiting hours, he walked through the lobby downstairs. A distraught man called out to him in a foreign accent to ask where he might find the hospital chaplain. It was long after visiting hours; a time when the chaplain would have been long gone for the day. But Phil told the man that he was a pastor and asked if he could help him. The man's wife was in a coma upstairs, dying. He wanted prayers to be said for her. The man was Muslim. Phil is a Christian. But still the man wanted Phil to accompany him to his wife's bedside. So they went up to the wife's room where the man's wife lay breathing her last troubled breaths, surrounded by a dozen or so loved ones who crowded into the room for that moment. Phil told those present that he was not a Muslim but a Christian. Phil then proceeded to care for the dying woman and her family as God cared for them. "Which way is Mecca?" he asked.

The husband pointed in a precise direction and Phil began to pray facing Mecca, as a way of acknowledging the importance of Mecca for this Muslim family and showing them his respect. He said to that family that God was there in the room with them as well as in Mecca. The family agreed, and received God's love from this Christian as he proceeded to tell them that God was there with them to care for them and their loved one. Together they prayed that God would receive the spirit of the one who was to die, and that God would sustain each of them in love and bind them closer together as a family in the difficult days ahead. They also offered thanks that the one who was dying would still be with them, even in death, in the power of God's love.[4]

God's love for all of us binds us together even in our religious differences and we can do no less than love each other. Nazarene theologian Michael Lodahl states it this way: "Simply put, the God who is Love would never say 'Enough!'" [5] For God so loved the world. God's love is indeed a radical love that calls us to a radical discipleship that is not always easy, but always necessary.

Growing up on my family's farm meant growing up next door to a man named Julio. We called him Don Julio out of respect for his age, but also out of great fear, for you see Don Julio was an evil man, a mean-spirited old goat! On school days we would walk down the gravel road that ran right in front of his house to get to the bus stop trying not to bring attention to ourselves for Don Julio took great pleasure in pelting us with stones as we walked by. Some mornings he would arise and block that gravel road so that my father and my uncles couldn't get to work for it was the only way off the farm. Only heaven knows what would make Don Julio so angry that he would risk our livelihood and his access to friendship.

One night my mother sent me on an emergency errand to my grandmother's home right beyond Don Julio's house. I didn't want to go, not because of the darkness of night, but because of Don Julio. I had good reason to fear. Just at the point that I thought I had traveled beyond Don Julio's grasp I felt the sharp, cutting pain of his horsewhip upon my arm and heard his cackle as he enjoyed my pain and fear. He was an evil man.

At the age of twenty-one when I was about to leave the farm to go to seminary, Don Julio sent word that he wanted to speak to me before I left. I remember turning to one of my sisters and a cousin and saying to them that I wasn't going alone to see Don Julio. They would have to go with me, and so the three of us went to Don Julio's. To our surprise he was most gracious, offering us cool drinks and cookies. I thought, "Oh my, this man is going to poison us!" But no, he had a request and I would need to live in order to fulfill his request. His request was that as I went to seminary, would I please remember him in my prayers. It was not what I expected. I told him that I would pray for him and we left. I confess that I did not pray for him often for the very memory of him was disturbing to my spirit. At some point I quit praying for him all together, but God did not release me from my pledge.

In my fourth appointment as a pastor I was sent to a congregation only ten miles from our family farm and thus ten miles from Don Julio. He was by then an old and sickly man. My mother would keep me informed of his declining health and encourage me to pray for him. "Oh, mother," I would say to her. "Why do you want to pray for that evil man?" She would remind me of God's transforming love. "And besides," she would say, "it's your job, you're a minister!" Thank God for Christian mothers who keep us on the path of righteousness!

Don Julio continued to decline and eventually he was moved to a hospice care unit. One afternoon Don Julio's wife called me. She told me that Don Julio was near death. The doctors could not explain his hanging on to life. His soul was restless, she said, and he had asked her to call me. Would I come? I remember a silence and a struggle within me before I could say that I would go, but I did finally say that I would be there within the half hour.

I went, trying to gather my thoughts, thinking about what I would say to him. None of the words of comfort I was so used to dispensing to persons facing death seemed to be appropriate. When I got to Don Julio's bedside he was struggling. His voice was weak but he didn't need his voice for his eyes spoke for him—he was terrified. I took his hand and was taken aback by the strength of his grip, and he would not let go. I said a few superficial words and then just stood there unable to offer anything else. It was dusk and I was looking out the window of his room when suddenly I saw a gust of wind and felt it blow within the depth of my soul and then I knew. In that moment I knew what I had to say to Don Julio.

Leaning close to his face I said to him, "Don Julio, God loves you." Then from a place within me, unknown to me, I heard my own voice saying, "And I love you, and my family loves you." And then it happened. Don Julio's face softened, his hand became gentle in mine, and tears began to wash away the terror in his eyes. I asked his wife to take his other hand and we prayed him into heaven, I am convinced of that. This was God's compassionate mercy at work. When we finished praying and commending Don Julio's spirit to God's care I felt that my own life had been set right and I experienced the incredible lightness of God's own peace. Through love the Spirit of God had transformed us all.

One day on an airplane I saw the documentary movie about Emperor penguins living in the Antarctic cold; *The March of the Penguins,* it's called. The beautiful, melodious voice of Morgan Freeman guides one through it. He starts by saying that it is a story of survival, but more than that, he says, it is a story of love, and like most love stories it begins with an act of utter foolishness. For God so loved the world that God gave God's Son that the world might be redeemed from sin to freedom, transformed from death to life. Now that is utter foolishness, the greatest foolishness, for it is the story of the greatest love! The apostle Paul is right:

> For the message about the cross is foolishness to those who are perishing, but to us who are being saved it is the power of God ....for God's foolishness is wiser than human wisdom....
> (1 Corinthians 1:18, 25a)

Are we willing to trust the wisdom of God? Trust that the love we have known in Christ Jesus has the power to transform our lives, the life of the church, and even the whole wide world? It can be, for God loves the world, holds us all in his loving arms, and gives us the incredible, transforming power of Christ himself for all eternity. This is the foundation of our faith as Christians.

6 Believing is Seeing

In the Gospel According to John, chapter 1:29-42, John the Baptist proclaims, "Here is the Lamb of God who takes away the sin of the world!" How could John have known that about Jesus? Perhaps he had seen him enough to say that Jesus was a good man, a wise teacher, but to say that Jesus is the Lamb of God who takes away sin, and not just the sin of Israel, of a little tiny community, of a few people, but the sin of the whole world! That was quite a declaration, an audacious statement, to say the least. It's confounding, especially since John the Baptist himself says that "I myself did not know him…" Yet, he is so sure that Jesus is the Lamb of God, the long-awaited Messiah, that he says it not to his family, not to a few close friends, not to those who followed him, but to the political leaders of his time, the priests and the Levites, to the entire world around him.

When John the Baptist says that he did not know Jesus, he is not saying that he had no knowledge of Jesus for they were from the same family. What is true is that John does not fully know who Jesus is until the Holy Spirit descends upon Jesus in the form of a dove in his baptism affirming that Jesus is the Lamb of God, the Messiah, the Savior of the world. Even then John has to trust the revelation of the Holy Spirit. He doesn't know all that will come because of Jesus, but he trusts that through Jesus, God reveals all of God's mercy, justice, and love. We have an advantage over John the Baptist, and that is that, through the witness of countless Christians over the centuries, we have received the good news of Jesus who has shown us the love of God. Yet we may still ask, "Is it possible to see Jesus among us?" What we learn from John the Baptist is that *believing is seeing*.

John the Baptist believed in God's promise of the Messiah; he believed in God's faithfulness. He believed and thus when the Holy Spirit reached down and touched him he was ready to see and saw Jesus right before him. Seeing Jesus among us is a gift of the Holy Spirit, given to all who believe.

Not so long ago I served a parish in Albuquerque, NM, among the poorest of the poor. Several congregations had joined together to try to reach out with the good news of Jesus Christ to a neighborhood in that community known as the "war zone" because of its deeply embedded violence, a violence born of poverty. We began our ministry in this area of Albuquerque by reaching out to the children. There was one child in particular who caught my attention because he was so very bright. He was also among our most mischievous and unruly children. But one day an incredible thing happened. After an Epiphany pageant that he participated in he came to me and said, "I want Jesus to live in me." Led, I believe, by the Holy Spirit, I said to him, "then follow Jesus." Lo and behold this child of about ten years of age began to show signs of believing in Jesus and following him. He became more attentive in Sunday school, requested a Bible, and began to volunteer to pray when we gathered in worship or sat at table for food and fellowship. It was quite an amazing transformation. I did not know how amazing until one very difficult evening.

That night I received a frantic call from his mother. Two of her older sons had gotten into a fight in the neighborhood and a neighbor boy had been stabbed to death. Her sons had been arrested and charged with murder. She asked, "Would I come and pray with her and her family?" I went immediately. There in their tiny, dark apartment I invited the family to gather in a circle for prayer. It continues to be one of the most difficult prayers of my ministry. But as I led us in prayer, that little boy who wanted Jesus to live within him, kept saying in almost a whisper, "Thank you, Jesus." When we finished praying I looked up and saw that little boy with a tender smile upon his face and then heard his incredible witness as he said to all of us, "My brothers will be all right because I know Jesus will be with them." Believing in the mercy of Jesus even on that dreadful evening he could see that Jesus would be with his brothers. Believing is seeing God at work among us. Believing in and thus seeing Jesus in his life, this child trusted and followed Jesus and blessed his family through dark times.

Believing and thus seeing God in Christ Jesus, John the Baptist followed Christ and invited others to do the same. Among the first to respond were Andrew and his brother Simon Peter who quickly wanted to know all about Jesus. Jesus' response to them and to us on this day is, "Come and see." Through their belief in Jesus those early disciples were gifted by the Holy Spirit to see Jesus in the fullness of who he is and what he does for all of us then and even now.

John the Baptist's witness is the inspiration of a beautiful liturgy that unfortunately we Protestants have forgotten or use all too infrequently. That liturgy is called the "Agnus Dei" which means the Lamb of God. The words are these:

> O Lamb of God, that takest away the sins of the world,
> have mercy upon us.
> O Lamb of God, that takest away the sins of the world,
> have mercy upon us.

O Lamb of God, that takest away the sins of the world,
grant us thy peace.

Believing and seeing Jesus through the gift of the touch of the
Holy Spirit is not a small thing. It is not simply seeing Jesus in the
privacy of our small lives and our limited communities of faith.
Believing and seeing Jesus is about participating in God's incredible, great plan of saving the whole world from its sin, its misery,
and its self-inflicted pain. Remember the words of the prophet
Isaiah as he believed in God's great mercy and saw the coming of
Jesus. Isaiah saw into the future with God's own eyes when he says
of Jesus:

> It is too light a thing that you should be my servant
> to raise up the tribes of Jacob and to restore the
> survivors of Israel; I will give you as a light to the
> nations, that my salvation may reach to the end of
> the earth.
>
> (Isaiah 49:6)

God's plan is to save the whole world; behold the Lamb of God
that takest away the sins of the world, giving us mercy, and granting
us peace. Do we believe enough to see that day of global redemption, universal mercy, and worldwide peace? One who believed unto
seeing was Martin Luther King Jr.

We particularly remember Martin Luther King Jr.'s historic "I
Have a Dream" speech. In his speech King speaks of his dream as
one "deeply rooted in the American dream." What we know of
King, however, leads us to know that his dreams were also deeply
rooted in his Christian faith. Living in the appalling injustice of
white privilege and American racism, King believed in God's mercy
and justice known to us through Jesus, and was able to lift his head

up and lift the hopes of people all over this country and even around the world, to a better day, to that day of God's redemption. "I have a dream," King proclaimed, "that one day…":

> …the sons of former slaves and the sons of former slave-owners will be able to sit down together at a table of brotherhood…

> …even the state of Mississippi, a state sweltering with the heat of injustice, and sweltering with the heat of oppression, will be transformed into an oasis of freedom and justice….

> …children will one day live in a nation where they will not be judged by the color of their skin but by content of their character…

> …every valley shall be exalted, every hill and mountain shall be made low, the rough places will be made plain, and the crooked places shall be made straight and the glory of the Lord will be revealed and all flesh shall see it together. [1]

Fortunately, and because of the sacrificial work of Martin Luther King Jr. and others like him, we have seen some of this grand dream become reality in our lifetime, but how could King have been able to see it in his lifetime, a time of violent racism without hope? I believe it was his faith in Jesus. Believing in Christ, King could dream and see what was possible because of Christ Jesus' mercy and justice. What is possible? Through God's great mercy in Christ Jesus we can confidently dream of and expect a day of mercy, of justice, and of peace, for behold the Lamb of God that takest away the sins of the world. Believing is seeing.

Belief of the seeing kind, though, is not an easy feat. Human sin often interferes as does human doubt. In his desire for us to believe unto seeing, Jesus himself helps us.

One day Jesus came to the region of Caesarea Philippi and he turned to his disciples and asked them, "Who do people say that the Son of Man is?" (Matthew 16:13). The disciples had heard the murmurings of the hearts of those who yearned for one who would come and bring healing to their bodies, hope to their spirits, and salvation to their lives. The question was an easy one, or at least the disciples thought it was. People had perspectives on who Jesus was. Some believed that Jesus was John the Baptist, while others thought he was surely Elijah. There were those who thought he must be one of the great prophets of old, and judging from the passion of his exhortations, perhaps he was Jeremiah. It is interesting that all the possibilities of who Jesus might be were dead men!

The person the disciples had come to know in Jesus was certainly not a dead man. He had taught them as no one else ever had, making the word of God come alive for them. They had seen him heal those beyond healing, multiply bread, and feed more people than they could imagine feeding in a lifetime much less on an afternoon in the middle of nowhere! Why, they had even seen him walk on water! Jesus was no dead man. Their hearts bore a different witness. That witness, though, needed a little coaxing so Jesus brought the question home, asking the disciples, "But who do you say I am?" (Matthew 16:15). Ultimately, it is, after all, a question that each one of us must answer for one's self.

As we study the Bible we find that Jesus is always more than willing to teach us about his identity. From the beginning of his ministry Jesus begins with full self-disclosure. In his first public action Jesus goes to his home synagogue in Nazareth and announces who he is. Employing the words of the prophet Isaiah he stands and boldly declares:

> The Spirit of the Lord is upon me, because he has
> anointed me to bring good news to the poor.
> He has sent me to proclaim release to the captives
> and recovery of sight for the blind,
> to let the oppressed go free,
> to proclaim the year of the
> Lord's favor.
>
> (Luke 4:18-19)

In case they had not understood that he was speaking of himself, Jesus stands firmly in the middle of the congregation in the synagogue and further states: "Today this scripture has been fulfilled in your hearing "(Luke 4:21b). How much clearer could he be?

Nothing is more self-revealing than to stand before one's family and friends, and those who may not think so favorably about us, and say to them that God's favor rests upon us in a unique and special way. Yet this is what Jesus said to those who were present in the synagogue in Nazareth, and it is what through Scripture he says to us today. While in retrospect Jesus seems abundantly clear, those present in the synagogue as Jesus declared that he was anointed of God needed to have Jesus explain what this all meant. If we are honest about our own understanding of the identity of Jesus in our own lives, we will confess that daily we find ourselves equally in need of having Jesus lead us in seeing clearly who he is for us. Fortunately, Jesus for the most part is patient and kind in helping us understand who he is.

As the disciples journeyed with Jesus in ministry, he spoke to them about himself. Sometimes he revealed himself through acts so amazing that they could not help but feel who he was, God's own self among them! How else could a woman bent over for eighteen years suddenly straighten up and walk tall (Luke 13:10-17)? How else could it be possible for the beggar Bartimaeus, blind from birth, to now see (Mark 10:46-52)? How else could the paralytic who required the help of friends to even get close to Jesus now be able to walk on his own all the way home (Matthew 9:1-12)? There was no doubt in those disciples' minds that God must surely be in Jesus. Knowing what this meant for their lives was somewhat more difficult so Jesus taught them through parables and sayings. People wanted to know what Jesus had to teach them. They gathered in great crowds to hear him; in homes, in open fields, even along the shoreline!

On a particular day Jesus sat by a lake and people hearing that he was there began to gather so that he could teach them. Soon the crowd was so large and so impossible to communicate with sitting by the lake that Jesus got into a boat and sat in it, using it as a podium from which to teach while the crowd stood on the shoreline. He taught them through parables, examples out of real life that they might be able to understand the mysteries of the reign of God. He said to them:

> The kingdom of heaven is like a mustard seed, that
> someone took and sowed in his field;
> it is the smallest of all the seeds, but when it has
> grown
> it is the greatest of shrubs and becomes a tree,
> so that the birds of the air come and make nests
> in its branches.
> (Matthew 13:31-32)

Jesus is the one who can explain the nature of God's kingdom, whose visible signs seem almost too small to see, yet the day will come when it will grow into a shelter for all of God's creation.

Jesus drew pictures of God's faithful work in nature and in the world. God's work among us is like a mustard seed, like a woman searching for a lost coin, like a father anxiously waiting for his lost son, like a precious pearl. God's holy activity in the world is indeed a work so precious that it is worthy of our investing all of our worldly possessions in order to obtain it (Matthew 13:44-46). In the process of drawing these powerful pictures for those who would listen, he was disclosing who he was. Jesus is the One who inaugurates the coming of the reign of God; the One who will lead us home.

The most frequent question I have been asked since coming to serve as a bishop of the church has been, "Where do you plan to lead us?" It is not a question that surprises me. It is a fair question, for, after all, I was elected to a position of leadership in the church. It is a question, however, that I believe misses the point of true Christian leadership. True Christian leadership is not about where we plan to lead the church, but rather where Christ Jesus is leading us and about being faithful to his leadership.

In John 10:1-10 we hear Jesus' voice speak to us about true leadership using the image of sheep and their shepherd. Jesus is speaking to the Pharisees, religious leaders of his day, and he is not immediately affirming. Instead Jesus berates the Pharisees for their failure to lead others to God. He compares those early religious leaders to thieves and bandits whose only intent is to kill and destroy the sheep. Unlike the true and faithful shepherd known by his sheep for his care, Jesus judges the Pharisees to be manipulative and self-serving. So how are we to lead so as not to fall into the error of the Pharisees? There is a classic Latin phrase that I believe captures how we are to lead. That phrase is, *in persona Christi.* John's story of the good shepherd provides us with insights into how we can be *in persona Christi.*

First of all the doorkeeper opens the door to the shepherd and the sheep hear his voice. Are we serving like the doorkeeper who opens the door to Christ Jesus, the Good Shepherd, enabling the sheep to hear his voice? Or are we closing the door, admitting only those who are like us, those with whom we are comfortable, those whom we like, those with whom we selectively choose to associate? Or are we holding the door wide open for all to experience the joy of hearing the voice of our Risen Lord? It is about being *in persona Christi*—persons and leaders of faith in the image of Christ.

I will never forget a visit I made, with leaders of the episcopal area I serve, to the Methodist Church of Mexico. We traveled to Agua Prieta, a border town in the Mexican State of Sonora. We went to join our brothers and sisters from Mexico in the dedication of a clinic that had been jointly built by Methodists from both sides of the Mexican-US border. We had a grand time cutting the ribbon for the opening of the new clinic, feasting at a table prepared by our Mexican Methodist brothers and sisters, and then joining together in a Spirit-filled time of worship. The worship was in Spanish, but I could tell that the ten or so English-speaking leaders from my episcopal area were feeling the presence of God's Holy Spirit in spite of the language barrier. Our Mexican brothers and sisters were so full of God's Spirit that they embodied Christ Jesus and opened wide the doors of God's presence for all of us.

The experience was so very real that during the prayer time one of the women from my area could no longer hold back, and though she understood absolutely no Spanish she proceeded to move to the front of the small sanctuary where we were worshiping and asked those who were leading prayer to pray for her. As I listened, I could hear our Mexican brothers and sisters praying for this English-speaking woman, calling her by name with a such a fullness of love that it was as if Christ Jesus himself were praying over her. Continuing to listen to this blessed prayer, I looked around at the other members of our English-speaking delegation and saw that there was not a single dry eye. Tears of incredible joy ran down our faces for our Mexican brothers and sisters were in that hour *in persona Christi* for us, and through them we could hear the voice of Christ Jesus, the Good Shepherd, calling us by name. Oh, if you and I could pray in that spirit and with that love for those around us who have yet to hear the voice of Christ Jesus calling them by name, our world would be a better place, and persons would know that we had led them to the Savior of the world.

To be *in persona Christi* for each other and for the world is to have the heart of Jesus. Jesus, the Good Shepherd, who, by his own account, came that we may all have life, and have it abundantly. Do our hearts yearn for abundant life not just for ourselves, but for every man, woman, and child upon the face of the earth? That is what it means to be *in persona Christi* with the very heart of Jesus. My good friend and colleague in ministry, Daniel Arguijo, was *in persona Christi* in my life.

The darkness of that early Epiphany morning belied the fact that it was a day of light; a day of remembering Christ Jesus who is the light of the world. It was in the darkness of that Epiphany morning that a hospital chaplain was called to a certain floor of the hospital where someone had just died. She went, gathering her thoughts of psalms and prayers for the family of the deceased. So focused was she on preparing to be at yet another bedside of death that she hardly noticed that she was alone in the elevator. Suddenly the elevator stopped on the requested floor, jolted a bit, and then released its doors.

As the elevator doors opened the chaplain was struck by a burst of unexpected light. It was after all barely five o'clock in the morning. She looked at the light fixtures up above, wondering if new neon lights had been installed since she had last been on this floor. Looking down a hallway all aglow she wondered, in fact, if all the lights had been changed. Walking down that hallway she had the sense that something beyond her comprehension had just happened.

As she passed the rooms of other patients, several who caught a glimpse of her called out to her, "He has died, hasn't he?" To which she would respond that he had. "Won't you open my door," one patient said, "that I might be able to see him go?" Yet another patient surprised her when he said, "Chaplain, open my door wide open so I can more fully see the light that's come to take him home."

It was my colleague in ministry, Daniel, who had just died. He had asked me to officiate at his funeral services when the time came. That time came much too quickly as he was afflicted and gone under the cruel power of a brain tumor before we could even grasp the grief of it all. But Dan never subscribed to the power of his illness. In and out of the hospital over several months, he would fight the illness in order to serve God and Christ Jesus. So, as soon as he was able, he would get up out of the hospital bed even if he had to drag his companion of hanging IVs, and go visiting the other patients on his floor, praying with them, comforting them, and assuring them that if they would just place their hope in Christ Jesus they would surely know that God was with them.

As I prepared funeral services for this incredible colleague, the hospital chaplain shared her story with me. It was, in fact, not unlike the story that Dan's spouse and children who were with him to his last breath, shared with me. I have always believed that Dan stood in the lineage of persons of great faith; faith so great that they can hope for life even in the grip of death, and are somehow able to convince others of life eternal—sight unseen!

Their names are many—Abel, Enoch, Noah, Abraham, Sarah, Isaac, Rebekah, Jacob, Rachel, Leah, Esau, Moses, Rahab, Gideon, Barak, Samson, Jephthah, David, Samuel, Isaiah, Amos, Jeremiah, Micah, Mary Magdalene, Steven, Peter, Lydia, Dorcas, Paul, and those others whom we hold in our own memories. Their names are many, and their stories are all different, yet all their lives and stories are rich in the witness that God is faithful to those who place their trust in him. Like a rhythmic song, Hebrews 11 reminds us of our ancestors in the faith:

— By faith they believed that from things invisible God had made the world;
— By faith Abel knew that God was a God of righteousness;
— By faith Noah built an ark to save his household in the time of judgment;
— By faith Abraham became a wandering Aramean for he could see before him that glorious vision of the city that has foundations, whose architect and builder is God;
— By faith Sarah turned from a world that ruled out all possibility of her having a child because of her age, trusting in God's promise of a son;
— By faith Moses abandoned wealth and privilege for he believed in God's justice;
— By faith the weak overcame the mighty; neither wild beasts nor raging fires could overcome them;
— By faith the faithful persevered, enduring insult, mocking, scourging, chains, imprisonment, and stoning; being sawn in two, killed with the sword, made destitute, afflicted, ill-treated, but always filled with the faith that could see beyond the sin and evil of this ordinary world.

Some years ago I had the great privilege of being in the presence of Dom Helder Camara, once the archbishop of Recife, Brazil. I had, by then, long been an admirer of his courageous and prophetic ministry. Named in 1964 as archbishop in Recife and Olinda in the poor northeast region of Brazil, he assumed his responsibilities as Brazil suffered a brutal military coup. Immediately this new bishop stepped forth as a strong advocate for human rights, for social justice, and for peace. Not many other church leaders joined him and soon he was red-baited, referred to as a Communist or as "the red bishop." Whatever persons chose to call him, he was, above all things, consistent; his life matching his preaching.

Rather than wearing a cross of gold or silver as is the custom of those in church power, his chest was adorned by a simple wooden cross. He abandoned the bishop's palace for a humble house. He opened the seminary doors to laypeople and even to women. In his actions and in his words he was truly a servant of the people. He was a simple man whose faithful and hopeful life threatened the powers to be.

During the time that he served as archbishop, Dom Helder Camara faced persecution and even death threats for standing with the poor of his diocese. For thirteen of those years he was banned by the military government from any public speaking, and the newspapers were not permitted to mention his name. His house was once sprayed with machine-gun fire and his offices were repeatedly ransacked. An assassin was even sent to his door. It is recorded that when Dom Helder answered the door and identified himself, the man was so undone by the sight of the frail and diminutive bishop that he abandoned his deadly mission, stating, "I can't kill you. You are one of the Lord's."

I, too, was taken aback by what I saw before me—a tiny old man who seemed to have but limited strength. But then he began to speak—words of deep faith from an obvious reservoir of interior peace and joy. By that time he had retired and seen his successor reverse much of his good work. Even then, he stood before us speaking to us of faith. He believed that if in every generation there could be so much as a remnant, a small community of those who keep hope alive and who are willing to risk security and comfort to seek the promised land, if only there could be such a community, the ordinary sin and evil of this world could be overcome by the extraordinary love and faithfulness of the One who is at work among us creating a better place. I want to be a bishop like Archbishop Dom Helder Camara, a member of that remnant that keeps hope alive; that holds up for the whole world to see visions of that better place, of the promised land, of that eternal homeland where God's love and holy purposes reign.

When the Tex-Mex singer Selena was murdered by the head of her fan club, I had no idea who she was, but my then five-year-old nephew John Paul did. Upon hearing the news of her death, he came running into my arms as he choked back his sorrowful tears saying, between sobs, "They've killed my Selena, they've killed my Selena." I tried to comfort him not knowing who he was mourning, but seeing his obvious pain over her death. Later, when Selena's family posthumously released a collection of her songs, I bought the CD, feeling somewhat out of touch with the world around me and wanting to better connect with my five-year-old nephew.

It's a wonderful CD with all the typical Tex-Mex themes of unrequited love and betrayal. But right in the middle of the CD is the real gem. It's a short but passionate song that I almost missed, but I'm glad I didn't. I wish I could sing it, but singing is not my gift so my efforts to translate the song's words will have to suffice. It says:

> If we all love each other the world will change.
> And oh joy by day and oh joy by night.
> If we all love each other the world will change.
> Don't tell me anything more about war and problems; Tell me you're going to live today so that tomorrow is worthy of hope.
> If we all love each other the world will change...[2]

Selena was in her early twenties when she was violently murdered. She died young but she died a Christian who could see what lay ahead. Now she sings to us from that great cloud of witnesses of faith—if we all love each other the world will change. We in the church all too often think that only through our preaching does God show God's own presence in the world. It is a sign of our arrogance and our tendency to attempt to box God into our comfort zones. But I do not lose hope for the church.

I believe that you and I can also see what lies ahead for we, too, have known the faithfulness of God. Is there one among us who cannot say with the prophet Isaiah that God has strengthened us, and helped us, and upheld us with his victorious right hand (Isaiah 41:10)? Or who is unable to take the words of the psalmist as his or hers and say boldly,

> The Lord is my shepherd, I shall not want; he gives me rest, he quenches my thirst, he restores my soul. The Lord leads me down the right path for his name's sake. The Lord comforts me and strengthens me even when I walk with death itself. The Lord sustains me with the food of his table even when others would wish my destruction. The Lord touches me with so much goodness and mercy that I cannot contain it all as much as I try.
> Though I live in this life now, I know that I will live in the house of the Lord forever. So I am not afraid for I have known God's enduring faithfulness.
> (Paraphrase of the Twenty-third Psalm)

As people who believe in Jesus, we are so very privileged. We are privileged to be able to stretch our hearts back to the psalmist and make his powerful, poetic words of faith ours, and yet also stretch our hearts forth to the great cloud of witnesses who have gone before us and who strengthen us by their lives and their eternal hope. Yet even more, we are blessed to know in our living "the pioneer and perfecter of our faith, who for the sake of the joy that was set before him endured the cross, disregarding its shame, and has taken his seat at the right hand of the throne of God" (Hebrews 12:2), namely Christ Jesus.

In Christ Jesus our hope is made complete. Our living and our dying are not in vain when for the sake of Christ we "lay aside every weight and the sin that clings so closely, and let us run with perseverance the race that is set before us" (Hebrews 12:1) being *in persona Christi*, and keeping our sights set on Jesus and Jesus alone.

Endnotes

Chapter 1: Opening Our Hearts to the Gift of Faith in Jesus Christ

1. Kenneth Cain Kinghorn, *John Wesley on Christian Beliefs: The Standard Sermons in Modern English*, vol. 1, 1-20 (Nashville: Abingdon Press, 2002), 38.
2. Ibid., 39.
3. Ibid., 39.
4. Donald W. Musser and Joseph L. Price, eds., *New and Enlarged Handbook of Christian Theology* (Nashville: Abingdon Press, 2003), 195.
5. Robert Ellsberg, *All Saints: Daily Reflections on Saints, Prophets and Witnesses for Our Time* (New York: Crossroad Publishing Company, 1997), 106.

Chapter 2: Faith in Jesus Over the Generations

1. Martin E. Marty, *A Short History of Christianity* (Cleveland: William Collins and World Publishing Company, 1959), 79.
2. Ibid., 79.
3. F. L. Cross and E. A. Livingstone, *The Oxford Dictionary of the Christian Church*, 2nd ed. (London: Oxford University Press, 1974), 870.
4. William H. Gentz, ed., *The Dictionary of Bible and Religion* (Nashville: Abingdon Press, 1986), 652.
5. Ibid., 736.
6. The United Methodist Church, *The United Methodist Hymnal: Book of United Methodist Worship* (Nashville: United Methodist Publishing House, 1989), 880.
7. Justo L. González and Zaida Maldonado Pérez, *An Introduction to Christian Theology* (Nashville: Abingdon Press, 2002), 84.
8. Ibid., 84.
9. Ibid., 85.
10. Ibid., 90.
11. The United Methodist Church, *The Book of Discipline of The United Methodist Church–2004* (Nashville: United Methodist Publishing House, 2004), 41.

12. Ibid., 45.

13. Ibid., 47.

14. The United Methodist Church, *The United Methodist Hymnal*, 881.

Chapter 3: Whose Faith Counts?

1. Robert McAfee Brown, *Reflections Over the Long Haul: A Memoir* (Louisville: Westminster John Knox Press, 2005).

2. The United Methodist Church, *The Book of Discipline—2004*, 74.

3. Ibid., 75-76.

4. The United Methodist Church, *The United Methodist Hymnal*, 597.

Chapter 4: Faith in Jesus in a Postmodern World

1. Jean-François Lyotard, *The Postmodern Condition: A Report on Knowledge* (Minneapolis: University of Minnesota Press, 1984).

Chapter 5: Envisioning a Faithful Church in a Postmodern World

1. Marcus J. Borg, *The Heart of Christianity: Rediscovering a Life of Faith* (San Francisco: HarperSanFrancisco, 2003), 139.

2. Bishop Kenneth L. Carder, "Conference That is a Means of Grace" (June 2006) http://www.umnexus.org/context.php?Article=100.

3. UMAction Briefing, *"Who Should Leave? UMAction Recommends: Highlights from 'Move Forward in Mission!' Statement"* and *"United Methodist Officials Lobby for Liberalized Immigration"* (Summer 2006), 2-3 http://www.ird-renew.org/atf/cf/{8548C466-4AF1-B844-9CE5165}/2006%2003%20UMA.PDF.

4. J. Philip Wogaman, *To Serve the Present Age: The Gift and Promise of United Methodism* (Nashville: Abingdon Press, 1995), 23-24.

5. Michael Lodahl, *God of Nature and of Grace: Reading the World in a Wesleyan Way* (Nashville: Abingdon Press, 2003), 190.

Chapter 6: Believing is Seeing

1. James M. Washington, ed., *A Testament to Hope: The Essential Writings and Speeches of Martin Luther King, Jr.* (San Francisco: HarperSanFrancisco, 1986), 219.

2. Selena, "No Quireo Saber," *Siempre Selena,* 1996, CD.

STUDY GUIDE
for

I believe in Jesus

BY Glory E. Dharmaraj

GENERAL GOALS FOR THE STUDY GUIDE

- To explore the main focus of this spiritual growth book, namely, the belief in Jesus.
- To hear Christian responses to Jesus' key question, "But who do you say that I am?" (Matthew 16:15).
- To study faith responses to challenges of faith in selected Gospel narratives; stories in the Acts of the Apostles; and experiences and documents of early martyrs and "apologists."
- To examine Christian responses to belief in Jesus through the lens of a variety of faith community contexts:
  — different social identities and locations;
  — encounters with the postmodern culture.
- To explore the impact of corporate belief in Jesus on local and global missions through the lens of different:
  — periods of history;
  — ecumenical conferences.
- To commit ourselves as believers to be co-workers with God in building an alternative world of shalom, which is characterized by peace, justice, harmony, and wholeness.

Each study leader must read the basic text, *I believe in Jesus,* by Bishop Minerva Carcaño.

As secondary resources, study leaders are encouraged to read *Post Modernism 101* by Heath White (Brazos Press, Grand Rapids, MI, 2006), and Leonard I. Sweet's *Post-Modern Pilgrims*: *First Century Passion for the 21ˢᵗ Century,* (Broadman & Holman Publishers, Nashville, TN, 2000), along with other resources.

METHODOLOGY

A central image I have selected is a round table in the center of the room. The notion of the church in the round is taken from Letty M. Russell's book *The Church in the Round: Feminist Interpretation of the Church,* which speaks about a vision of a Christian community of faith and struggle as it seeks to practice God's hospitality.[1]

SESSION 1

THE CHURCH AS A ROUND TABLE AND IDENTITY THEFT

GOALS

To study the belief in Jesus in the context of different social identities and locations, especially that of migrant labor.

To explore Christian responses to Jesus' question, "But who do you say that I am?" (Matthew 16:15).

REQUIRED MATERIALS

- The Bible for every participant.
- The basic text, *I believe in Jesus,* by Bishop Minerva Carcaño, for every participant. The book may be ordered from the e-store; www.missionresourcecenter.org or by mail from the Mission Resource Center, 1221 Profit Drive, Dallas, TX 75247. It is available also in Spanish and Korean language editions.
- A round table with five chairs around it. One chair is broken. (Write "BROKEN" on that chair, if the brokenness is not visible.)
- One basket of tomatoes and a second basket of picked cotton (symbolically, a basket of cotton balls).
- A salt shaker.
- An unlit candle covered with a cardboard box or some other cover.
- A bowl of water.
- Four cups of water.
- Index card for each member of the class.
- Color markers, newsprint, newsprint stand, and non-toxic magic markers; United Methodist Women's "PURPOSE" posters in English, Spanish, and Korean languages on the wall. (Check

beforehand to see if putting up posters is allowed.)

For the Facilitator's use, a copy of *The United Methodist Book of Discipline—2004* (if the 2008 version is not available when you do this study).

OPENING PRAYER (2 minutes)

God, who calls us out by name, be with us and equip us as we begin the task of a new study. In this session we are going to learn how to keep focusing one eye on the gospel and the other eye on the "least of these." Help us engage our whole self in your mission, as we strive to walk this journey together, as a community of people committed to your calling and your mission. In Jesus' name, we pray. **Amen**.

COMMUNITY BUILDING: SOCIAL IDENTITY AND SPIRITUAL IDENTITY

(30 minutes. Facilitator gives the directions listed below to the participants.)

1. Take an index card. On one side of the card, please write the word **FROM.** On the other side of the card, write the word **TO**.

2. On the **FROM** side of the card, write answers to the following questions: What is your social identity? How do you identify yourself socially? [Social identity refers to one's gender, race, ethnicity, class, religion, age (young, middle-aged, old), ability and disability, etc. Other subdivisions may be added to this basic list, if suitable.]

3. On the same side of the card, write or draw symbols of where your ancestors come from.

4. On the **TO** side of the index card, please answer this question: Recall one significant moment in your life when you felt called to be a child of God. When and in whose company did it happen?

5. Write or draw a symbol of that affirmation.

6. Lifting up your card, briefly share with the rest of the class your name and what you have written under your social AND spiritual IDs.

FACILITATOR:
ONE EYE ON THE GOSPEL AND THE OTHER EYE ON THE REALITIES OF "THE LEAST OF THESE"

(Explains - 3 minutes)

What the participants have done is to locate themselves in their social identities as well as in their identities as children of God. It is a bifocal seeing.

This spiritual growth study requires us to fit ourselves with a trifocal faith lens which sees through the lens of:

• One's social identity;
• One's child-of-God identity;
• Our neighbors' faith stories, which are rooted in family, social, and cultural contexts.

Social identity is where you come from; that is, your roots. It can be called "home" with a small "h." In addition, you have another identity; that is, the child-of-God identity. Bearing this identity, you are engaged in a journey toward God, who is your Home ("H" capitalized). Bearing each other's burden, we are called upon to make a community journey together as people of God, with all our differences, yet with one eye on the gospel and the other eye on the realities of "the least of these." (The Facilitator collects all the IDs and places them on the table.)

BRANDED BY BAPTISM AGAINST IDENTITY THEFT (A meditation in a skit form. Four readers are needed.) (15 minutes)

FACILITATOR:

Let us ask ourselves some key questions before we do this skit on "Branded by Baptism Against Identity Theft":

• What is Jesus' social identity?
• His family identity?
• How do others perceive his social identity?
• What kind of family identity does Jesus prioritize?
• Who is Jesus' family? (Matthew 12:46-50)

Let us meditate on the identity of Jesus, as I read these Scripture passages:

FACILITATOR (Reads aloud):

Luke 3:15-17, 21-22
John 10:40-42
(The four readers go to the table and sit on the chairs around the table.)

READER 1:

It is good to sit at a round table to talk about identities, especially Jesus' identity. See these ID cards of our sisters and brothers on this table. I am fascinated by the gospel stories which talk about Jesus' identity. The Holy Spirit hovers over Jesus and alights on Jesus in the form of a dove. It seems that love has the final word in this event, as always: "You are my Son, the Beloved;" (Luke 3:22). In this decisive event, Jesus' hour has come to begin his ministry. Also, this is the time of his call to give himself for others. At this key moment, God reinforces Jesus' identity as God's child. This is Jesus' ID card, "You are my Son, the Beloved."

READER 2:

I wonder how many of us here can say that such a thing has happened to us lately. I mean, such a breathtaking sound-and-sight event telling us that we are children of God?

READER 3:

I agree. But, for most of us, the affirmation comes in a less dramatic way. It comes, nevertheless. The Bible tells us that whoever does the will of God is a member of Jesus' family (Matthew 12:50). Jesus resets definitions of identity for his followers. It is done in terms of a radical *kinship* model. The true identity of a person, in this new definition, is the *child-of-God self.*[2] One's true self, in this sense, is a child-of-God self. It is up to you to say, "I believe in Jesus," and to do his will, I suppose.

READER 4:

I have a feeling Jesus already knew his identity even before such a dramatic thing happened. As a twelve year old, didn't Jesus tell his distraught mother, who had been searching for her missing son, that he was on his Father's business? (Luke 2:49). I think the key issue here is not the sound-and-sight thing. It is Jesus' priority of his child-of-God identity above all other worthwhile identities such as his Palestinian Jewish identity, hometown identity, family identity, kinship identity, and so on. The child-of-God identity is Jesus' true identity.

READER 2:

Then why is identity such as an issue in our church?
(At this point, the Facilitator asks the class to name some of the identity-related issues in the local churches from which the participants come. The Facilitator writes short phrases from the responses on the newsprint, puts up that page of newsprint on the broken chair, or tapes it onto the broken chair at the round table.)

READER 3:

I am sure there are broken places in our own lives and the church has broken places, too, in relation to the issues we have just named. Within the church itself, there is a great need for healing and reconciliation. At least we need to start from something about which we all agree.

READERS 1-3:

Yes. Then we can agree to disagree on other things later on.

READER 1:

Let me try. We all agree that in baptism we receive our identity as a Christian. Recalling the baptismal vow is one way to strengthen our identity as the body of Christ. It helps us to remember, in a fresh way, what it is to die with Jesus and to rise again with him into one body of Christ.

• Baptism represents means of grace.
• Baptism is a doorway to a sanctified life (Philippians 1:9-11).
• Baptism is a representation of new birth in Christ.
• Baptism is a sign of regeneration.
• Baptism is not something we do.
• Baptism is given to us. We are given something which we can not achieve on our own.
• Baptism means inclusion in God's community.

READER 2:

I like sermons in sound bites.

READER 4:

I am afraid what I am going to say may not be in sound bites. It is important to recall our baptismal vow and renew it. The Bible tells us that Jesus himself walked back to the Jordan banks to gather himself. The context is poignant. When he is questioned on his identity as the Messiah and is rejected by the leadership, he goes back to the place where he was baptized (John 10:40). For me, it is a beautiful and poignant moment. Jesus may have remembered the magnificent sight of the dove and the affirming voice of God, "You are my Beloved Son."

It is time for us also, maybe, symbolically and in memory, to go back to the place of our baptism and renew the baptismal vows. We are a water-washed and Spirit-born people. Lest there be any identity theft by lesser loyalties, let us walk back to reclaim our baptismal identity. We are a people branded by baptism against identity theft.

READER 2:

You know what? I like the one sound bite, at the very end of your otherwise preachy stuff. That is, **we are a people branded by baptism against identity theft.**

(All four readers of this skit go back to their seats.)

LITANY: A SACRAMENTAL WALK BACK TO OUR BAPTISMAL IDENTITY (5 minutes)
(The leader holds a bowl of water in her hands and reads the allotted portion. If the study is done in a church, stand near the baptismal font.)

Leader: Let us recall our own baptism as we read the following litany.

Leader: In the scorching heat of our theological disputes,
All: Let us take a sacramental walk back to our baptismal identity.
Leader: In the dead winter of our being that saps our emotional strength and moral resilience,
All: Let us take a sacramental walk back to our baptismal identity.
Leader: In the midst of life's demanding responsibilities and challenges,
All: Let us take a sacramental walk back to our baptismal identity.
Leader: Pilgrims within and pilgrims without, let us take a hallowed walk,
All: For it is our inheritance of the Spirit, the wealth of our well-being.
Leader: Co-traveler, will you share your travel experience in this journey?
All: Fellow traveler, can I hold your hand on our way back when needed?
Leader: Friends, let us hold each other up. It is right and wholesome to walk the walk that way with Christ's strength.
All: It is right and wholesome for us to strive to live as one baptized body this way. Amen

(The leader places the bowl of water on the table. Four persons bring water in cups and each pours the water into the bowl.)
Bearer of cup 1: This water is from my own well, from the North. I offer this as a symbol of my spirituality.

Bearer of cup 2: This water is from my own well, from the South. I offer this as a symbol of my spirituality.

Bearer of cup 3: This water is from my own well, from the East. I offer this as a symbol of my spirituality.

Bearer of cup 4: This water is from my own well, from the West. I offer this as a symbol of my spirituality.

Leader: We walk sacred walks from our spiritual wells to this place of gathering. Each one of you brings your own faith to this table, often shaped by different histories, different cultures, different experiences. We all come to this table as children of God, seeking to build bridges across our many differences.

HYMN: "I Was There to Hear Your Borning Cry," (stanzas 1-3), #2051, *The Faith We Sing.* (5 minutes)

SILENT READING (5 minutes)
The Facilitator gives time for all the participants to read chapter 1, paragraphs 1-3, in Bishop Minerva Carcaño's basic text, if they have not read it already.

THE GOD OF THE SHARECROPPER'S FARM
Exercise on "YES," "NO," "DON'T KNOW" (10 minutes)
(The Facilitator can either use all participants or pick four participants from the class and ask them to form a single file, standing in the middle of the classroom. Each has to answer the following questions by saying: "Yes," "No," or "Don't know." If one feels the answer is yes, that person has to move to her or his left. If the answer is no, the person moves to the right. If the person does not know the answer, she or he stands in the middle. Decisions are made individually and not as a group.)

1) Is it necessary to understand a culture from the points of view of the people from that particular culture?

2) Would Jesus be considered an "ethnic" person, if he were to live in the US today?

3) We should not acknowledge our racial and ethnic differences, but erase our racial and ethnic differences, if we are to live harmoniously in the US.

4) Was God present on the sharecropper's farm before the missionary came to the farm with the gospel?

5) The missionary's task is to learn what God is already doing there on the sharecropper's farm.

6) The missionary's task is not to introduce the farm workers to a world from which the farmhands are absent. In other words, the missionary's task is to introduce to the farm laborers the God who knows the pain and sufferings of the laborers.

7) Analyzing racial, economic, cultural, political, and other sources of oppression is important for a missionary before he or she goes out to minister in a particular place.

8) God still continues to call people in their broken places and sites of struggle to turn Godward in Christ through grace.

9) Spirituality and social action should not be separated in one's personal and collective spiritual journey.

(Answers for the study leader are given in Appendix 1.)

FACILITATOR:

Each believer brings his or her social, cultural, and family contexts to his or her faith understanding. When it comes to spirituality, different people **drink from their own wells**.[3] They should and they must. Symbolically, four different persons brought waters from their wells and poured these waters into the bowl on the table.

MIGRANT LABOR AND THE "GOD-QUESTION"
(15 minutes)
(Place a basket of picked cotton and a basket of tomatoes on the table. In place of cotton, the Facilitator might want to use a basket of cotton balls, or even pictures of picked cotton.)

FACILITATOR:
In the basic text, the basket of farm-picked cotton and the basket of farm-picked tomatoes represent the migrant labor of the economically poor Hispanic laborers, including children.

Particularly in the story of Bishop Minerva Carcaño's childhood memories, the pickers are marked by "ethnicity." They are mainly Hispanics, including her grandparents, parents, and herself.

(The Facilitator elicits from the total class responses to the following questions:)
a) What are some of the images and associations that come to your mind when you hear the word, "ethnicity" or "ethnic person"?
b) What are the positive and negative things associated with the word "ethnic" in the US context?
c) Does the love of ethnic food translate to liking ethnic persons? Can one like ethnic food and be indifferent to the plight of ethnic persons who eat that food?
d) Talking about the word "ethnic," which comes from the New Testament Greek word "ethnos" or *ethnikos,* Josiah Young III says, "To consider those who are ostensibly different from ourselves as "ethnikos," would banish their suffering—and their blessedness—from our part of the world and from our consciousness so that we can hoard abundant life. But Jesus came to say that life is to be shared,

and not hoarded."[4] Do you agree or disagree with the statement? Why?

ONE EYE ON THE GOSPEL AND THE OTHER EYE ON THE LEAST OF THESE—THE "GOD QUESTION"

The majority of us who are doing this spiritual growth study are "non-poor people." Let us imagine ourselves sitting around this table in the center. Before we eat the fruits of labor, it is helpful to keep one eye on the gospel and the other eye on the "least of these." On behalf of the "least of these," ask the questions, "How are the children of the farm laborers doing? How are the least of these doing?" They are questions most of us who are not poor need to ask before we eat from our bounty.

Jim Wallis, an evangelical and a faith-based activist, says when we deal with social and economic decisions and policies, we must ask what he calls the "God Question." That is, "How are the kids doing?"[5] This is a litmus test in mission. How are our children doing? How are the children of the least of these doing? *"How are the children doing?"* was the theme of the ecumenical Advocacy Days in March 2007 in Washington, DC.

Often those of us who belong to middle-class churches, or even just those of us who are not poor, are caught up in limited and limiting visions of justice. John Cobb Jr. says, "We are caught up in a destructive system, and we find that even our will to refuse to identify with that system is mixed with the desire to enjoy its fruits. None of us are innocent, either in intention or behavior."[6]

We are caught in contradictions and moral dilemmas. But the "God Question" places God's vision of God's justice before our eyes.

WHY SHOULD ONE CONFESS ONE'S FAITH?

(Small group discussion for questions below—10 minutes; then share for another 10 minutes.)

QUESTIONS:

Why should we confess our faith individually? Corporately?

Why should we confess our faith around the table?

Whose voice is absent when we confess our faith?

Is it the laborer's voice? If so, can you resolve to lift up the plight of the voiceless as you confess your faith in God, in Jesus?

WHO DO YOU CONFESS? (Matthew 16:13-16)

"But who do you say that I am?"

Who is Jesus to you?

Who is Jesus to you in light of what we have discussed today?

BENEDICTION:
LITANY ON "PASS THE SALT, PLEASE" (10 minutes)

[As persons are asked to stand around the table, the Facilitator removes the cover over the candle, lights the candle on the table, puts the salt in a dish for people to touch, and keeps the bowl of water ready on the table for use. The Facilitator lifts up the symbols of light and water which are on the table, and says that these are powerful symbols in the church tradition. Lifting up the salt, the Facilitator says that, in the ancient Hebrew tradition, salt was a symbol of the eternal nature of God's covenant with God's people. With its power to strengthen and preserve food from decay, salt stands for the removal of all impurity and hypocrisy on the part of God's people, and for their willing offering of themselves to God. Jesus himself invites God's people to be the "salt of the earth" and "the light of the world." Jesus says, "You are the salt of the earth; but if salt has lost its taste, how can its saltiness be restored?"

(Matthew 5:13). Jesus also says, "You are the light of the world. A city built on a hill cannot be hid" (Matthew 13:14).]

Leader: Lord, you invite us to come to your table of grace on your sacred merit, for the name of your table is Grace.

All: **The name of your table is Bounty.**

Leader: The name of your table is Mercy.

All: **The name of your table is Healing.**

Leader: Now I invite you to come up with more names for God's table. "The name of your table is_____" (The Facilitator opens the liturgy to the class for a few minutes.)

Leader: God of Mystery, we acknowledge that all our naming cannot fully describe your table.

All: **We pray for those who can name your table silently or in words,**

Leader: We pray for those who are not able to name your table yet. Your name is still "God-with-us."

All: **You are God-with-us, at the table, touching us, healing us, and asking us to touch each other in a healing way.**

Leader: We pray for all those whom we exclude from this table.

All: **We pray for all those who come to this table timidly and stealthily.**

Leader: At the table, you invite us to be the "salt of the earth."

All: **At the table, you invite us to pass the salt to each other.**

Leader: "Pass the salt, please," so that I can be seasoned in your love.

All: **"Pass the salt, please," so that I can offer myself as nourishment in mission to others.**

Leader: God of Plenitude, grant us the gift of salt in our lives, so that we can fully taste your passion for the kingdom of God, the rule of justice, peace, and wholeness.

Leader: We recall our baptism, and we covenant with you, Holy God, to be the "salt of the earth" so that we can embody your presence in the world.

All: **We recall our baptism, and we covenant with you, Holy God, to be the "salt of the earth" so that we can embody your presence in the world.**

Leader: God of life, you are the breadth of our love.

All: **Washed by your streams of love, we offer ourselves to you, in the midst of our brokenness, and ask you to heal your broken people, and mend the broken creation.**

[The Facilitator asks each participant to come to the table and take a pinch of salt with one hand. Participants are invited to dip their fingers of the other hand in the water in the bowl, and to make a sign of the cross on their own foreheads recalling their own baptism. While doing so, the group sings the rest of the verses of "I Was There to Hear Your Borning Cry," (stanzas 4-7), #2051, in *The Faith We Sing*.]

LEADER:

People of God, in baptism we receive both our identity and mission. As children of God, we are called to be in God's mission. We celebrate here the security of being God's children. We also celebrate God's call to each of us to engage in God's mission. Go, therefore, in God's name. Celebrate your identity and your calling.

HOMEWORK:

• Read chapters 1 and 2 in the basic text by Bishop Minerva Carcaño.

• Ask three volunteers to be prepared to read the first person narrative by Joanna found in Session 2, pages 135-141.

- The Facilitator divides the class into four small groups and asks each group to choose a person to tell the following persons' stories in the form of a first person narrative. (Each of the four storytellers will have five minutes each.)

  Group 1: First person narrative by Mary Magdalene. Read Luke 8:1-3, John 19:25, and Luke 24:1-10.

  Group 2: First person narrative by Cornelius. Read Acts 10:1-48.

  Group 3: First person narrative by Peter. Read Acts 10:1-48.

  Group 4: First person narrative by Lydia. Read Acts 16:11-15 and Acts 16:40.

- Each participant should come prepared tomorrow to either share a faith story of his or her own or that of a family member. At the end of the narration of the story, each should also be able to summarize the key element of the faith story in three to four words.

SESSION 2
FAITH SEEKING UNDERSTANDING

"I do not seek to understand so that I may believe, but I believe so that I am to understand; and what is more, I believe that unless I do believe I shall not understand."

Saint Anselm, 11th century[1]

"Third World theologies are *missionary* theologies, whereas First World theologies are not. Many Third World Christians seem to realize that they live in a missionary situation, in the fullest sense of the word. Perhaps this is so, first, because the poles between which those theologies move are not those of belief and unbelief or theism and atheism, but rather those of life and death or God (of life) and idols (of death)."[2]

GOAL
To study faith responses to challenges of faith in selected gospel narratives, stories in the Acts of the Apostles, experiences and documents of early martyrs, "apologists," and *The United Methodist Book of Discipline.*

REQUIRED MATERIALS
- Round table with a cross on it.
- Copies of the Apostles' Creed and the Nicene Creed. (See *The United Methodist Hymnal*, #880, #881, and #882.)
- Quilt fabrics. (If the Facilitator cannot get fabric materials for the quilt-making activity, use assorted colored papers or letterheads with borders and large poster paper on which to patch these pieces of papers to make a quilt of faith stories.)
- Glue sticks.

OPENING HYMN: "We'll Understand It Better By and By," (stanzas 1-2), #525, *The United Methodist Hymnal.* (3 minutes)

PRAYER (Sung in unison) (2 minutes)
Let us all pray the prayer of an eleventh-century theologian, Saint Anselm:
"Lord, I am not trying to make my way to your height, for my understanding is in no way equal to that, but I do desire to understand a little of your truth which my heart already believes and loves."[3]

BIBLICAL REFLECTION
Who are you, Jesus, anyway? (Luke 7:18-23, John 11:17-27). (10 minutes)

READER 1:
Listen to the story of a key believer. Listen to the query of John the Baptist from his prison cell.

This is the context of the story. Herod Antipas married his own niece and sister-in-law, Herodias. Her daughter, Salome, lived with her in the new court. You know the rest of the story, don't you? How the one man who dared to criticize that marriage was killed? Yes, John the Baptist refused to keep his religion in the isolation of the wilderness.

READER 2:
John the Baptist sent word from the prison to Jesus, "Are you the one who is to come, or are we to wait for another?" (Luke 7:19). During moments of instability and change, our faith may flounder on key understandings of who we are and whose we are. Standing for one's convictions amid life's cruel turns of events, and rapid

131

change of circumstances, may force us often to have second-guesses and questions.

READER 1:

In one such moment, John the Baptist asks of Jesus, "Are you the one who is to come, [as our Messiah] or are we to wait for another?" Are you the one to save us from the Roman Empire?

READER 2:

Maybe it is a coded language from the prison cell where John was languishing since he was put there for condemning Herod for his adultery. Jesus does not give a straightforward response to John's question. Jesus tells the disciples of John, "Go and tell John what you have seen and heard: the blind receive their sight, the lame walk, the lepers are cleansed, the deaf hear, the dead are raised, the poor have good news brought to them. And blessed is anyone who takes no offense at me" (Luke 7:22-23).

FACILITATOR:

Take a moment of silence, turn in your Bible to Luke 7:22-23, and read this same passage silently. Answer to yourselves: Does John feel and experience a silence and omission in this list concerning prisoners being set free? John's head is soon to be cut off at the whimsy of the dancing step-child of Herod and her mother. What are some of the true challenges of faith? What are some of the testing times in your faith? (Brief sharing time.)

HYMN: (Sung in unison) "We'll Understand It Better By and By," (stanzas 3-4), #525, *The United Methodist Hymnal.*

READER 3:

Let us gather our thoughts around another story in the Gospel;

that is, Martha's faith statement, "I believe…" (Reader 3 reads aloud John 11:17-27.)

READER 4:

Jesus takes time, in the midst of a death in the beloved family of Mary, Martha, and Lazarus, to strengthen the faith of the sisters. Jesus also reorients Martha's faith by affirming, "I am the resurrection and the life." Martha instantly gives her faith statement: "I believe that you are the Messiah, the Son of God." This extraordinary confession of faith takes place just before Lazarus is brought back to life by Jesus.

FACILITATOR: (Compares Peter's confession with Martha's.)

Faith still seeks understanding. One does not have to *understand* fully in order to exercise one's faith.

Christianity itself is a *revealed* religion. Christian faith is founded on a core belief that God has revealed God's self through Jesus the Christ. There is an element of mystery to faith in this self-revelation. Exercising faith is not a one-time effort. It is an ongoing, continuing conversation between God and the child-of-God self. It is an ongoing conversation between God and the church, God and the world. As the hymn writer says, "We will understand it better by and by."

SHARING THE FAITH STORIES THAT SUSTAIN YOU–QUILT-MAKING ACTIVITY

(The Facilitator distributes quilt fabrics or papers equally to each of the four groups. Each group answers the following questions and works on its quilt material. If, at the local church level, the group is too small to engage in this activity, ask participants to write on pieces of paper and post them on the wall, or place them on the round table, in any design they like.) (30 minutes)

(a) What is ONE key element in Bishop Carcaño's narration of the stories of faith of her mother and grandmother? Summarize in three to four words. (5 minutes)

(b) Briefly share a story of faith to the person on your right in your group. This can be a story about someone in your family or someone you know, or it can be from your own personal faith journey. This story should be one which still sustains you. You should be able to narrate this story within four minutes to your neighbor, and also come up with a three- to four-word summary of your story. What does this story have to teach you? Examples: courage in adversity, laughter amidst hardships, standing on God's promises, etc. Use your own words to summarize your story. Do not use more than three to four words. (8 minutes)

(c) (The total class, divided into four groups, engages in this activity.) As a small group, select a couple of phrases from among the shared faith summaries. Paint/write some of the selected words on pieces of fabric or paper. You can also draw symbols of faith to represent the key element in the story of faith. Start the process of painting or writing. If you do not have time to finish it, please do it in your spare time. (12 minutes)

(d) Are there common key elements among the stories that you shared in your group? Pick out just ONE element. One person from your group will share this with the total group. (5 minutes)

(e) Find some free time after the class and tie the quilt fabrics with the ribbons found in the packet. If there are not enough holes in the fabric pieces to tie the ribbons, try to make one more hole in the middle of the top and bottom of each fabric piece, and tie one more piece of ribbon through the holes. If you are working with paper, glue pieces of papers on a poster paper to make a quilt. Add more pieces if necessary. Be ready to place the quilt on the round table when you come to Session 3 or Session 4. (Choose a person who can coordinate this.)

RESPONSES TO FAITH IN JESUS AND CHALLENGES TO FAITH–FIRST PERSON NARRATIONS (10 minutes)

(a) (The story of Joanna who has seen Jesus and experienced his deeds. Three volunteers read the three parts given below.)

Part 1: JOANNA'S BELIEF STATEMENT

I am Joanna. I am one of the Resurrection Women. But you do not hear much about me. I was one of the women who helped Jesus and his disciples with my resources. You do hear about me in the Gospel According to Luke 8:1-3.

I, too, am a disciple who followed Jesus and his disciples through towns and villages. I left my home, my slaves, AND King Herod's court society to follow Jesus. That is why you do not hear much about me. When King Herod's senior royal officer's wife follows Jesus—that is an event for national gossip.

I remember Herod Antipas marrying his own niece and sister-in-law, Herodias. Her daughter, Salome, lived with her in the new court. You know the rest of the story, of how the one man who dared to criticize that marriage was killed. Yes, John, the Baptist. The prophet refused to keep his religion in the isolation of the wilderness, insulated from the world.

John the Baptist dared bring his witness to the court circles in Galilee. Herod's court circle is one of glamour and lust, wealth and deception, manipulation and servitude. Salome danced through it all, on that seductive and fatal day.

I heard about her dance through my husband, Chuza. The Herods are not unaccustomed to creating killing fields.

John the Baptist paid the ultimate price for witness to power in his day—death by violence, caused by Herod Antipas.

The father of Herod Antipas, known as Herod the Great in history, ordered the massacre of thousands of innocent children under the age of two. Bethlehem itself became a killing field. You know the other side of the story of Christmas—a state-sponsored terrorist act, a killing spree by Herod the Great.

As an infant, Jesus escaped the terrorist act of Herod the Great as the Holy Family fled to Egypt. But many other male children under the age of two were not so fortunate. There were civilian deaths in the sacred story.

Well, I, Joanna, needed healing—healing of my own mind and body; healing from memories of trauma and violence; and healing from an empty court society, with its fear of the Roman Empire's overriding influence, and its inability to address it, due to its own moral crisis from within.

The prophetic voices which pointed out these corroding moral crises were stifled. But, but...

Jesus healed me. He taught me that God cares even for the lilies of the field and the sparrows that sell for a penny in this strange economy of ours.

However, I chose to support God's economy with my inheritance and resources. I shared my wealth with Jesus and his disciples.

To follow Jesus is a risk-taking mission. Often I was identified as someone who once belonged to Herod's party, a highbrow woman, a former member of Herod's court, standing in solidarity with Jesus, a traitor!

To follow Jesus is a revolutionary thing. Jesus challenged my allegiances.

Therefore I took to the road, following Jesus all the way from Galilee to Jerusalem, and then to the site of Jesus' resurrection, desolate, outside the city.

You see, Herod Antipas, too, journeyed from Galilee to Jerusalem. Our paths ran parallel. Belief in Jesus the Christ, or disbelief in the same, determines one's course in life.

Part II: MEMORIES OF JOANNA, A WOUNDED HEALER
Herod followed the road of indecision and violence, standing in solidarity with Pilate, the Roman governor, and helped deliver Jesus to his death. Herod and Pilate walked the imperial road of violence and state-sponsored terrorism. It is strange that Herod and Pilate forgot their long-standing enmity and forged friendship and reconciliation at the expense of Jesus.

I, Joanna, walked to the foot of the cross and witnessed Jesus being tortured and killed as a common criminal.

I went to keep an early morning vigil at his tomb with spices for embalmment. Instead of the dead Jesus, I saw the Risen Savior.

I went there as a spice-bearing woman, and came away as a bearer of faith memories.

My journey led to the Risen Christ. You see, there are two journeys, King Herod's journey and mine. King Herod, too, traveled all the way from Galilee, his jurisdiction, to Jerusalem, the center of the Passover ceremony, as well as the seat of Roman power in that area.

I followed Jesus from Galilee to Jerusalem, to the site of the cross. Our journeys are different. Our moral maps are different, with different foci and different views of terror and peace.

Herod's reconciliation with Pilate led to the murder of Jesus.

I carry these difficult memories of terror and violence.

I have difficulty fathoming how enemies become friends in order to condemn an innocent man.

Reconciliation is a good concept.

But...

The reconciliation of Herod and Pilate, the reconciliation of religious leadership and political authorities, in order to condemn the innocent and subject them to torture exposes the potential for a lurking violence in religion. The good news of the gospel is that God, in Jesus Christ, is the author of reconciliation in a different way.

For true reconciliation is transformative. True reconciliation is healing, since true reconciliation is truth telling. Therefore, two streams of memories are grounded in my mind to this day: the difficult memory of Jesus' death, and the healing memories of his resurrection.

The church even celebrates this death and life embrace of memory. "The night in which he was betrayed…"

The all too familiar Eucharist call for memory.

The Christian God is a betrayed God. The Christian God is a crucified God. This betrayal and this crucifixion bring to the church's memory all the "crucified peoples" of the world.

The healing memory of the Resurrection further restores the victim, the poor, and the oppressed, for reconciliation must begin with the victim. The victim has to initiate the reconciliation process, and not be rushed into it by the perpetrators.

Part III: JOANNA, A BELIEVER AND A WOUNDED HEALER
The victim, Jesus, initiates this process immediately after his resurrection, in spite of the wounds still in his physical body. The restorative process brings the victim, the perpetrator, and the community together for further healing, restitution, and renewal of the social, communal, and national psyche.

I, Joanna, am a witness to this memory of the early church—the healing memory which comes from God, the author of reconciliation. To be more apt, God, the victim-author of reconciliation.

Restorative memory does not forget the past. It has offered me a chance to walk with Mary Magdalene; Mary, mother of James;

Mary, the mother of Jesus; and a whole community of women who see the past differently now.

Forgiveness is an important step towards healing the wounds. It reduces the deadly effect of the wounds and fosters the building of a new community. It enables a different relationship with the past memory of hurt, terror, and victimization. Having a community of women with you who see differently helps.

For me, this is a moral high ground of Jesus, the Christ, and the Jesus movement. These are some of my travel memories. You have your travel memories, I am sure.

The oral record of Jesus' movement, as I know it, is a record of Christianity as a minority religion in a majority culture. It is yours to figure out, in your context, how decisions taken on behalf of peace, life, and justice make a difference in the world.

The Bible talks only about terrorism from above—that is, terrorist acts brought about by the powerful to oppress the powerless.[4]

There may come a time when people may experience terrorism from below. That is, terrorist acts from those who lack power but who nevertheless engage in acts of terror, mainly to send out a message to the powerful.

But some of the prophets of old functioned, with their travail of vocation and calling, in the midst of terror from all sides, as prophet Jeremiah would put it, still calling for justice, peace, and humility in the public square and in the personal sphere.

May we, too, never forget our prophetic calling in the midst of terrorist acts. May we be undergirded by the strength of our own sense of who we are, whose we are, and with whom we stand in solidarity.

I, Joanna, am a bearer of these memories. The community of women with whom I walk this journey brings gifts along the way:

The gift of new naming for transformed memories; the gift of looking death and devastation squarely in the face and writing resurrection into them; and the gift of finding meaning through it all. The psalmist calls it a song in the night (Psalm 42:8).

My fellow traveling women and men, let us continue to gather strands of music of unity and diversity, for God who is in the midst of it *all*.

Through it all—we *are Resurrection People because we believe in Jesus the Christ. Belief in Jesus leads us to radical action.*

GROUP ACTIVITY
(Representatives of Groups 1-4 share their first person narratives.)
(20 minutes)
Group 1: First person narrative by Mary Magdalene: Luke 8:1-3, John 19:25, Luke 24:1-10.
Group 2: First person narrative by Cornelius: Acts 10:1-48.
Group 3: First person narrative by Peter: Acts 10:1-48.
Group 4: First person narrative by Lydia: Acts 16:11-15, 40.

CHALLENGES TO FAITH AND ARTICULATION OF CREEDS (15 minutes)
(Silently read the Apostles' Creed and the Nicene Creed. See *The United Methodist Hymnal,* #880, #881, and #882. Also read pages 23-29.)

In many instances in the early centuries of Christianity, the church had to take a stance against false teachings, heresies, and even the interference of the state in the affairs of the church. **Note: Christology is a term which means an individual's or the church's understanding of Jesus as the Christ.**

(a) What were some of the Christological concerns discussed in the original formulation of the Apostles' Creed?

(b) What were some of the Christological concerns discussed in the original formulation of the Nicene Creed?

(c) Was there a consensus when the Apostles' Creed and the Nicene Creed were formulated? Why/Why not?

(d) When you confess your faith through the Apostles' Creed in a gathering of believers, what are some of the key beliefs that you confess?

(e) When you confess your faith through the Nicene Creed in a gathering of believers, what are some of the key beliefs that you confess?

(f) Why is it not enough to confess faith individually? What is the need for common confessions of faith such as the Apostles' Creed and the Nicene Creed?

(g) Why should local United Methodist churches affirm their faith through the Nicene Creed and the Apostles' Creed in The United Methodist Church? See *The United Methodist Hymnal*, #880, #881, and #882.

(h) Does it mean that The United Methodist Church is a creedal church? Why/Why not?

ATONEMENT THEORIES (15 minutes)

(a) Ransom Theory

Roughly from the fourth to the eleventh centuries, this theory had a major impact. According to this theory, Christ's death on the cross is a "ransom," an expiation, or a sacrifice, for our sins.

The Atonement as a "transaction with the devil" was repudiated by Gregory of Nazianzus. He asks, "Was it paid to the evil one? Monstrous thought! The devil receives a ransom not only from God but of God...To the father? But we were not in bondage to him....And could the Father delight in the death of his Son?"⁵

QUESTIONS

Is Christ's death on the cross a ransom to the devil or a payment to God? What do you think? Is there a third way of understanding beyond this?

(b) Satisfaction Theory of Anselm

Anselm, an eleventh century theologian, made a shift in the understanding of the Atonement of Christ. Anselm says, "Let us first consider what sin is, and what satisfaction for sins is...To *sin* is to fail to render to God what is His due. What is due to God? Righteousness, or rectitude of will...And what is satisfaction? It is not enough simply to restore what has been taken away; but, in consideration of the insult offered, more than what was taken away must be rendered back...The satisfaction ought to be in proportion to the sin...And this cannot be done except there be a complete satisfaction made for sin; and this no sinner can make. Satisfaction cannot be made unless there be some One able to pay to God for man's sin something greater than all that is beside God...Now nothing is greater than all that is not God, except God Himself. None therefore can make this satisfaction except God...Death was an offering that He (Christ) could make as of free will, and not of debt...What greater mercy can be conceived than that God the Father should say to the sinner—condemned to eternal torment, and unable to redeem himself—'Receive my only Son and offer Him for thyself,' while the Son Himself said—'Take me, and redeem thyself.' And what greater justice than that One who receives a payment far exceeding the amount due, should, if it be paid with a right intention remit all that is due?"[6]

QUESTION
How do Justo L. Gonzáles and Zaida Maldonado Pérez help us understand Anselm's concept of Atonement? (See pages 29-31 in chapter 2.)

ATONEMENT THEORIES CONTINUED (10 minutes)
(a) What does the Atonement theory of New Humanity say?
(b) What is the Wesleyan belief regarding Atonement?
(c) What does Christ's Atonement mean to you?

"I BELIEVE" STATEMENTS (Optional)
(a) The Nobel Prize lecture Elie Wiesel delivered on December 11, 1986, in Oslo, Norway, begins with the words, "*ANI MAAMIN*, I believe." Wiesel, a Jewish theologian, philosopher, and a holocaust survivor, goes on to say, "I believe in the coming of the Messiah...I believe in the hope of the future, just as I believe in the irresistible power of memory." He ends his Nobel Prize lecture saying, "Ani maamin—I believe—that we must have hope for each other also because of one another. And Ani maamin—I believe—that because of our children and their chil-

dren, we should be worthy of that hope, of that redemption, and of some measure of peace."[7]

(b) Naim Ateek, director of the Sabeel Ecumenical Center for Liberation Theology in Jerusalem, said, at the conclusion of the Lenten "Solidarity Visit" on Sunday, April 6, 2003, that when he looked at his people, Palestinian people, and the people of Iraq, "It is not resurrection that we are experiencing daily but crucifixion." Then Ateek stretches out his theological hands to embrace Jon Sobrino, a South American theologian, and quotes the latter, saying:

> At the center of the Christian faith lies the assertion that Jesus of Nazareth...died by crucifixion...The cross...embodies the authentic originality of the Christian faith...In recent theology of resurrection, looking to it as the paradigm of triumphant liberty and the joy of living which was lost in the cross. In short, theology has tended to sidestep the task of reflecting on the cross itself.[8]

CLOSING LITANY:
GOD, THE GATHERER OF OUR FAITH STORIES

Leader: God, the sustainer of our faith, we have come this far by faith.

All: **Redeeming God, you have clothed us with your saving grace.**

All: (Sung response)
**We have come this far by faith,
Leaning on the Lord;
Trusting in His holy word,
He's never failed us yet.
Oh, can't turnaround,
We've come this far by faith.**

Leader: God, gathering our faith stories, we have come to your presence.

All: **Gather us into one body.**

Leader: God of Many Colors, each of us is a piece of fabric in your skillful hands.

All: **God of Unity, we have come this far by faith, asking you to weave us into your multicolored body called the church.**

All: (Sung response)
We have come this far by faith,
Leaning on the Lord;
Trusting in His holy word,
He's never failed us yet.
Oh, can't turnaround,
We've come this far by faith.

Leader: Gather us, with our joys and pains, into your fold of mercy, your quilt of grace.

All: **Maker and Mender of our lives, design our lives as you choose.**

Leader: Each of us is a piece of fabric in your hands, O Master Designer; gather us together, as you desire.

All: **Gather us into One Whole called your church, across the land, across the globe.**

All: (Sung response)
We have come this far by faith,
Leaning on the Lord;
Trusting in His holy word,
He's never failed us yet.
Oh, can't turnaround,
We've come this far by faith.[9]

HOMEWORK

- Read chapters 3-4 in the basic text by Bishop Minerva Carcaño.
- Divide the total group into four small groups and give reading assignments from the *2004 Book of Discipline* (if the 2008 edition is not yet available). Group 1 will read "Scripture" under the Wesleyan Quadrilateral found in ¶104, pages 78-79. Group 2 will read "Tradition" on pages 79-80. Group 3 will read "Experience" on pages 81-82, and Group 4 will read "Reason" on pages 82-83.
- Ask the class to watch the video, "Post-Modern Pilgrims," available from Peter Sheldrup, 2716 Utter Street, Bellingham, WA 98225. (Phone number: 360-756-1094; website: www.peteralvar.com.)

SESSION 3
ACTING OUT OUR FAITH IN JESUS IN A POST-MODERN CULTURE

"I call postmodernity an EPIC culture: Experiential, Participatory, Image-driven, and Connected."

Leonard Sweet [1]

"The true 'Quadrilateral' believer is not one who subscribes simply to a SERT methodology (Scripture, experience, reason and tradition)…When a multidimensional faith is lived synergistically and holistically, a biodance takes place between the heavens and the earth, the Creator and the creation."

Leonard Sweet [2]

GOALS
To examine Christian responses to belief in Jesus through the lens of a variety of faith community contexts:
—different social identities and locations;
—encounters with the postmodern culture

REQUIRED MATERIALS
A round table with a cross on it. Continue to keep the dish of salt on the table. Keep an unlit candle on the table. If the quilt is done, place it on the table. A portion of it can hang from the table. On the table, place colored lenses/eye glasses cut out of construction paper. Have enough copies of the Wesleyan Quadrilateral from *The Book of Discipline* for small group reporting. Also, have enough copies of "The Glossary of Selected Theological Terms" (in the back of the book, after endnotes) for each person.

OPENING HYMN (3 minutes)
"Many Gifts, One Spirit," #114, *The United Methodist Hymnal.*

BIBLICAL REFLECTION
"But who do you say that I am?" (Matthew 16:15, I Peter 3:15)
(10 minutes)
Facilitator asks a volunteer to read the Scripture passages, and asks the group, "Who do you say that Jesus is?" The response to this question shapes our response to our engagement in mission.

Throughout Christian mission history, the church's response to Jesus' question, "But who do you say that I am?" has led to different actions and impacts on communities and nations. See Appendix 2, "20th Century—Decades of Christian Mission" by Robert Harman.[3] In the last session, the class will get a chance to work on this chart in a small group activity.

Being ready to give an account of one's hope:
"but in your hearts sanctify Christ as Lord. Always be ready to make your defense to anyone who demands from you an accounting for the hope that is in you" (I Peter 3:15).

(a)   What does this Scripture passage mean?
(b)   "We are answerable to the world for our belief and our actions. We have the obligation to explain to people what we believe and what we do not believe, why we act in a certain way and not in other ways. Christians are not obliged to do what others tell us but we are under obligation to explain our convictions and actions."[4] This is an interpretation by Raymond Fung of I Peter 3:15. Do you agree? Why? Why not?
(c)   In small groups, share how you would give an account of your Christian belief today.

149

AN AFFIRMATION OF FAITH: "THE HEARTHHOLD OF GOD"

By Glory E. Dharmaraj

(Read in unison) (7 minutes)

We believe in God the Almighty who hovered in love over the primal chaos and void, and uttered creation into existence.

We believe in the magnificent signature of God's image in every human being, signed in infinite variety, sewn in multicolored splendor, and woven into multiplicity of cultures.

We believe in the revelatory signature of God in Jesus the Christ who came to restore God's image in every human being.

We believe in Jesus who came to open our eyes so that we may see each other into God's image.

We believe in Jesus who came to open our ears so that we may hear each other into community.

We believe in Jesus who came to open our hearts so that we may love each other into God's gift of love for the "other."

We believe in the Holy Spirit who never seems to stay put, but relentlessly births hope at the edges, in broken places, and in the dead-ends of our lives.

We believe in the Holy Spirit who pushes the church to reach out to the margins, and who continues to urge the church into close listening and fresh witnessing to God's grace.

We also believe that one day, fully restored into God's image, we will all feast in God's presence in the Hearthhold of God. We believe in the glorious reunion of God's family members, when God will set up a feast for us.

We believe in the final bursting forth of the great orchestral music of the church and the cosmos inviting us all to God's dance, to be gathered into the very bosom of God's love.

Until then, we will work for the fullness of the in-breaking of God's kingdom among us.

Until then, we will build bridges of healing and reconciliation, justice and wholeness, restoration and harmony, among all God's peoples.

As a foretaste of that final reunion, we will offer ourselves to set up hearthholds of God here and now, for the "least of these," and create dance spaces for the hurting and the heavy laden.

Therefore, we commit ourselves every day to the day of God's great feast in the Hearthhold of God,[5] when, fully healed and fully restored, all God's children will be swung into God's dance into the very bosom of love. **Amen.**

DIFFERENT CONTEXTS AND VOICES AT THE TABLE
(30 minutes)
(Divide the entire class into seven small groups. Each group chooses a reporter. The Facilitator gives each reporter a different colored lens/eye-glass made out of construction paper. The paper eye-glass should be big enough for each group to write down their key points. Give ten minutes for the small groups to write down the answers to the following questions.)

Group 1: Reads the paragraph that talks about Rosemary Radford Ruether (pages 46-47).

Group 2: Reads the paragraph on James H. Cone (page 47).

Group 3: Reads the paragraph on Gustavo Gutiérrez (pages 47-48).

Group 4: Reads the paragraph on Cecil "Chip" Murray (page 49).

Group 5: Reads the paragraph on Robert McAfee Brown (pages 49-50).

Group 6: Reads the paragraph on Elisabeth Schüssler Fiorenza (pages 51-52).

(All the groups will answer the same questions given below on a paper cut out in the shape of an eye-glass.)

QUESTIONS FOR ALL THE GROUPS:

(a) What is the key contribution or approach to the understanding of God by the particular theologian?

(b) What kind of "oppression," if any, does the particular theologian address? In other words, what is the CONTEXT of the theologian?

(c) Is there one phrase that can be used to sum up the contribution of the person? If so, what is it? Example: Feminist theology, Womanist theology, Liberation theology, African-American theology, etc.

[Each reporter gives a three-minute presentation, places her/his report on the round table, and walks back to the seat.]

DIFFERENT LENSES, DIFFERENT CONTEXTS, DIFFERENT WAYS OF DOING THEOLOGY

[The Facilitator discusses the commonalities and differences among the various theologies, and the context of each theology. Distributes the handout: A Glossary of Selected Theological Terms (pages 176-177).]

FACILITATOR:
How does *The Book of Discipline* define "theology"? What does it mean to you to do theology? [The Facilitator elicits individual responses based on chapter 3 in Carcaño's basic text (pages 43-56).] (5 minutes)

WHAT ARE THE CHARACTERISTICS OF POSTMODERN CULTURE? (45 minutes)
(a) The Facilitator enables the participants to explore the different characteristics of modernism and postmodernism in Bishop Carcaño's basic text.
(b) What are some of the key characteristics of the postmodern age, according to Carcaño, as described in chapter four?
(c) Two persons present a reading on modernism and postmodernism. Modernism and postmodernism are often reduced to simple categories of thought. The following reading seeks to capture some of the differences between modernism and postmodernism, while acknowledging that there is more to be learned about modernism and postmodernism.

The Facilitator defines modernism as a worldview and a mindset which were prevalent in the West roughly from a period between the seventeenth and mid-twentieth centuries. This is the period which broke with the medieval period in history.

Postmodernism is a worldview and a mindset that began in the mid-twentieth century.

The Facilitator asks participants to listen carefully to the dialogue, informing participants that at the end of the dialogue they will be asked to answer the question: **"What are some of the strategies needed for being an effective church in the postmodern period; that is, in today's culture in North America?"** (Two persons are needed for the reading.)

A DIALOGUE BETWEEN MODERNISM AND POSTMODERNISM:

MODERNISM: My name is MODERNISM.
POSTMODERNISM: My name is POSTMODERNISM

M: My town's name is CENTER.
PM: My town's name is POLY-CENTER.

M: I am proud of being an independent, autonomous, and stable SELF.
PM: I am proud to be a socially constructed SELF. I am formed by social forces such as parents, schools, community, and even political forces.

M: I am a RATIONALIST.
PM: I am INTUITIVE.

M: I arrive at OBJECTIVE TRUTH through REASON.
PM: There are no such things as OBJECTIVE TRUTH and OBJECTIVE REASONING. Everything is RELATIVE to where you are and what your experiences have been. I am contextual, and I look through several perspectives.

M: I am proud to be complete.
PM: I am humble enough to be partial.

M: I believe in INDIVIDUALISM.
PM: I believe in RADICAL PLURALISM.

M: I see REALITY through the eyes of DOMINANT stories.
PM: I see REALITIES through the eyes of MULTIPLE lenses.

M: I wonder how you READ YOUR BIBLE?
PM: I wonder how you READ YOUR BIBLE?

M: There IS a proper way of reading when it comes to the BIBLE. I seek to find a UNIFIED MEANING in the Bible.
PM: In MY reading of the BIBLE, I see a VARIETY OF MEANINGS AND INTERPRETATIONS depending on the reader's social location, race, gender, cultural background, and other identity markers

M: I pity your inability to see the UNIVERSAL MEANING in the Bible for all times and all cultures.
PM: I beg to differ. You ought to see PARTICULAR MEAN-INGS for particular cultural settings in the Bible.

M: You must be caught up in the IDENTITY POLITICS in the church. You are at the mercy of DIFFERENCE AND DIVERSITY.
PM: On the other hand, I CELEBRATE DIVERSITY AND DIFFERENCE.

M: You don't look beyond your identity and difference, do you? You FRAGMENT people, fragment history, AND fragment the church itself by your IDENTITY POLITICS. WHAT IS TRUTH for you then?

PM: I would reframe your question and ask, WHOSE TRUTH? Truth implies a lot of power. The basic question for me is WHOSE TRUTH? All your grand stories are written by DOMINANT GROUPS, from their dominant points of view. THAT IS WHY I would argue that the stories of the subordinate groups are equally important.

M: RELATIVISM is your other name then? You are FLUID.
PM: You are FIXED and FROZEN like the food in my freezer.

M: I am for ABSOLUTES, even ABSOLUTE TRUTH.
PM: I am for RELATIVISM, even MORAL RELATIVISM.

M: You need to choose one thing over the other. There is only an EITHER-OR POSITION.
PM: There is no either-or for me. I believe in BOTH-AND POSITIONS.

M: "I THINK, THEREFORE I AM."
PM: I FEEL, THEREFORE I AM.

M: You must be a teary-eyed, bleeding HEART.
PM: You must be a cold and aloof "HEAD" person.

M: I am sequential in my thinking. I believe in cause and effect.
PM: I am simultaneous. I am not reduced by cause and effect.

M: How circular!
PM: How linear!

M: You seem to wear round hats always!
PM: I notice you wear square hats always! In addition, you seem

to wear only a white lens for your eye-glass.

M: You seem to wear a multicolored lens. Often that baffles me.
PM: That is because I do not want to look through the same pair of eyes. Yours is a MONOCHROMATIC vision. Mine is a rainbow-colored vision.

M: You use big words! Let me ask you. Do you believe in Jesus?
PM: Do you?

M: YES. I believe in Jesus. Do you?
PM: YES. I believe in Jesus, too.

M: My church's challenge is to TELL THE GRAND STORY OF JESUS AND HIS LOVE.
PM: My church's challenge is to SHARE THE STORY OF JESUS IN THE MIDST OF COMPETING STORIES.

M: I believe there is only one Jesus Christ.
PM: I believe there is only one Jesus Christ.

M: I believe there is only ONE CHRISTIANITY.
PM: I believe there are MANY CHRISTIANITIES.

M: MY NAME IS MODERNISM
PM: MY NAME IS POSTMODERNISM.

(d) **DVD**:
"Post-Modern Pilgrims" (Show a five-minute clip.)
Discuss the key characteristics of what it means to be in a postmodern culture. Discuss some of the new ways in which faith in Jesus can be shared in the postmodern culture.

GOSPEL AND POSTMODERN CULTURE:

The core message of the gospel remains the same. Jesus is the same yesterday, today, and tomorrow. The message of the gospel cannot be domesticated either by modernity or postmodernity.

In commenting on the relation between gospel and culture, Kosuke Koyama, a Japanese theologian, says that the gospel "cannot be completely adjusted, indigenized, contextualized, accommodated, adapted, re-symbolized, acculturated, inculturated, and incarnated to culture. The Gospel displays its authentic power in its refusal to be completely indigenized...A perfect indigenization is an idolatory of culture."[6]

WESLEY'S EYE-GLASSES: QUADRILATERAL (10 minutes)

(a) Divide the total group into four small groups. Give out copies of the "The Nature of Our Theological Task" from *The Book of Discipline.* Groups will be assigned the following questions.

Group 1: What does it mean to be "constructive" in our theological task?

Group 2: What does it mean to be both "individual and communal" in our theological task?

Group 3: What does it mean to be "contextual and incarnational" in our theological task?

Group 4: What does it mean to be "practical" in our theological task?

Remind each group of its homework for tomorrow for Session 4:

Group 1 will give a report on one of the Wesleyan Quadrilaterals, "Scripture," from *The Book of Discipline.* See under "Our Theological Task" the subheading, "Scripture" (In *2004 Book of Discipline*, ¶104, pages 78-79).

Group 2 will give a report on "Tradition" (*2004 Book of Discipline,* pages 79-81).

Group 3 will give a report on "Experience" (*2004 Book of Discipline,* pages 81-82).

Group 4 will give a report on "Reason" (*2004 Book of Discipline,* pages 82-83).

The leader will be prepared to give a summary of "The Present Challenges to Theology in the Church" (*2004 Book of Discipline,* pages 83-84).

(On the table, the Facilitator places a lens/eye-glass made out of construction paper, with the word QUADRILATERAL written on it, saying that the ongoing struggle for The United Methodist Church is how to bring a holistic understanding and living of the Quadrilateral into our postmodern church, which often tends to live in a previous period, namely modernity.)

(8) CLOSING WORSHIP:
FROM CONFESSION LANGUAGE TO PERFORMATIVE LANGUAGE

Leader: The Bible is full of instances of the faith community's belief statements leading to their language of performance and commitment. For instance, the psalmist's belief in God's faithfulness leads the former to say, "I will lift up the cup of salvation and call on the name of the Lord" (Psalm 116:13). Remember the United Methodist hymn, #2164, in *The Faith We Sing,* where the singer says, "I'll be a living sanctuary for you." This is an instance of performance language. Now, let us gather our thoughts for the closing worship for this session:

Leader: Because we believe in Jesus the Christ, let us pray that
           our confessional language always leads to a language of

action, and then to the action itself.

All: **Because we believe in Jesus the Christ, let us engage ourselves in pledging anew to the renewal of our communities.**

(Sung response)

Lord, prepare me to be a sanctuary,
pure and holy, tried and true.
With thanksgiving, I'll be a living sanctuary for you.
("Sanctuary," #2164, *The Faith We Sing*)

Leader: Because we believe, we will unleash the life-giving forces in the prophetic tradition.

All: **Let us gather ourselves into life in its fullness in Jesus the Christ.**

Leader: Because we believe, we will share the newsbreaking story that God has come to transform our tomb-like existence into sanctuaries of service and worship.

All: **Because we believe, we will share God's newsbreaking story that angels still roll away stones.**

(Sung response)

Lord, prepare me to be a sanctuary,
pure and holy, tried and true.
With thanksgiving, I'll be a living sanctuary for you.

Leader: Because we believe, we are a Resurrection People set out to transform the world, in the name of Jesus.

All: **Because we believe that we are the bearers of the cup of salvation, we will work against all the forces that diminish human worth.**

Leader: We will work against all the forces that mar God's image in each and every human being.

All: **Together with God, we will challenge the systems that deny our neighbors fullness of humanity.**

(Sung response)
Lord, prepare me to be a sanctuary,
pure and holy, tried and true.
With thanksgiving, I'll be a living sanctuary for you.

HOMEWORK

• Read chapters 5-6 in the basic text.
• Read Acts 15:1-34 and John 21:1-14.
• Watch the DVD, "Through the Corridors of Mission." Stock number M3023, $4.99. It is available from the Mission Resource Center, www.missionresourcecenter.org or 800-305-9857.

SESSION 4
CHRISTIAN BELIEF LEADING TO MISSION PRACTICES

"The church exists by mission, just as fire exists by burning."

Emil Brunner[1]

"For theology, rightly understood, has no reason to exist other than to critically accompany the *missio Dei*."

David Bosch[2]

GOALS

• To explore the impact of corporate belief in Jesus on local and global missions, through the different periods in twentieth-century history, and through the lens of different ecumenical conferences.

• To commit ourselves, as believers, to be co-workers with God in building an alternative world of shalom which is characterized by peace, justice, harmony, and wholeness.

MATERIALS REQUIRED

Place olive oil on the table in a couple of cups or large cup-like seashells into which to pour the oil. If possible, also have olives on the table. Have a candle and the dish of salt on the table. Each participant will need a Bible, and a copy of Appendix 2 (the chart on 20th Century—Decades of Christian Mission).

OPENING WORSHIP (5 minutes)

HYMN: "As a Fire Is Meant for Burning," #2237, *The Faith We Sing.*

BIBLE STUDY (15 minutes)

JERUSALEM COUNCIL: FAITH AND PRACTICE

(Turn to your neighbor on your right, and together share your responses to the questions given below, based on Acts 15:1-34.)

(a) What were some of the challenges addressed in the Council of Jerusalem?

(b) What were some of the methods employed by the members of the Council of Jerusalem which changed the course of mission to the Gentiles?

(c) How did they arrive at a consensus?

(d) What is the impact of the decision of the Council on the Gentile Christians?

(e) What is the role of gospel and culture taken into consideration, in the decision making of the Council of Jerusalem?

CHRISTIAN BELIEFS AND IMPACT ON MISSIONS IN THE 20th CENTURY

Divide the class into four small groups. Groups 1 and 2 discuss questions (a) and (b). Groups 3 and 4 discuss questions (c) and (d). (15 minutes)

Look at the chart in Appendix 2 on "20th Century—Decades of Christian Mission" by Robert Harman and answer the following questions:

(a) Pick up two themes from the decades listed by Robert Harman which you think are still relevant.

(b) What are some of the key verses in the Bible which inspire you to be engaged in mission today, in the last part of the first decade of the third millennium?

(c) How do different understandings of Christology (belief in Jesus) relate to diverse mission activities and ministries? Pick two examples.

(d) Formulate a relevant belief statement for today's church in the US, in the last part of the first decade of the third millennium. What kind of impact do you think this faith statement will have on the ways we do missions?

GIFTS FROM THE CHRISTIANS IN THE GLOBAL SOUTH (25 minutes)

(a) What was the gift offered to a group of Christians from the US, during their trip to Mexico, by the Christians in Agua Prieta, a border town in the Mexican State of Sonora? (pages 100-101 in the basic text.)

(b) What are some of the gifts offered to the churches in the US by the Christians in the Global South (developing countries) which you have experienced?

(c) What is the testimony of Dom Helder Camara, a former archbishop of Reclife, Brazil?

(d) Referring to the poor Christians of Sao Paolo and their role in evangelizing the rich, W. J. Milligan quotes a message from the Sao Paolo poor:

> "The poor, a believing oppressed people, announce and demonstrate the presence of God's Kingdom on their journey; in their struggle; new life—the resurrection manifested in their communities—is living testimony that God is acting in them. Their love of their brothers and sisters, their love of their

enemies, and their solidarity, show forth the active presence of the Father's love. The poor can evangelize because the secrets of God's Kingdom have been revealed to them."[3]

If you are not poor, how do the poor evangelize you?

FAITH AND SOCIAL JUSTICE RESPONSIBILITIES
(In small groups) (25 minutes)
(a) Belief in Jesus the Christ impacts and influences Christian missions, including social justice activities. How does Bishop Carcaño's belief in Jesus, and her own social and episcopal identities, lead her to take a stance on behalf of the immigrants?

(b) Do you agree with the following statement on being Christians? Why? Why not?
Jim Wallis, an evangelical and a faith-based activist, says, "The American churches are now in deep solidarity with the world-wide body of Christ and may have to choose between their Christian alliances and the demands and policies of their own government. We must learn to be Christians first and Americans second."[4]

(c) What are some of the controversial social justice challenges that polarize and divide The United Methodist Church? Name them. (Write these down and post them on the broken chair at the round table. Pick one key issue from among them and discuss possible ways of addressing this issue.)

FAITH AND SPIRITUALITY (5 minutes)
What can your local church provide to the "seekers" who feel that there is a "hole in their soul"? (According to a study commissioned

by United Methodist Communications, there is a new audience category identified as "seekers.")

These seekers experience a sense of discomfort or a "hole in the soul." These persons are between the ages of twenty-one to sixty who feel that there is something missing in their life. They seek meaning and purpose, and want to resolve emotional pain or frustration. Therefore, they search for something better spiritually in life. They do not attend a United Methodist church, but are willing and open to the idea of a church being a reasonable option to meet their needs.

Visit the website at www.ignitingministry.org in order to learn about the 2005 study done by Barna Research Group, Ltd.

CLOSING WORSHIP (15 minutes)

COVENANTING FOR MISSION
Voice 1: (Lifting up the dish of salt.) Hear the Word of God, as it is written in the Gospel According to Matthew 5:13. "You are the salt of the earth; but if salt has lost its taste, how can its saltiness be restored? It is no longer good for anything, but is thrown out and trampled under foot."

All: We believe in Jesus the Christ. Therefore, we covenant with God to be the salt of the earth.

Voice 2: (Lifting up a lighted candle.) Hear the Word of God, as it is written in the Gospel According to Matthew 5:14-16. "You are the light of the world. A city built on a hill cannot be hid. No one after lighting a lamp puts it under the bushel basket, but on the lampstand, and it gives light to all in the house. In the same way, let your light shine before others, so that they may see your good works and give glory to your Father in heaven."

All: We believe in Jesus the Christ. Therefore, we covenant with God, the Light of the World, that together, we are the light.

Voice 3: Hear the Word of God, as it is written in the Acts of the Apostles 1:8. "But you will receive power when the Holy Spirit has come upon you, and you will be my witnesses in Jerusalem, in all Judea and Samaria, and to the ends of the earth."

All: We believe in Jesus the Christ. Therefore, we covenant with you, O God, and with each other to be your witnesses, at home, in our neighborhood, among those considered our enemies, and even to the ends of the world. Gracious Savior, may we cross barriers courageously, trusting in the wideness of your mercy. Be it so. Amen.

LEADER: (Reads Hebrews 12:1-2.)

HYMN: "Sois la Semilla" ("You Are the Seed"), stanza 1, #583, *The United Methodist Hymnal.*

LITANY:
WE ARE OLIVES, PRESSED AND TRANSFORMED INTO OIL

(The leader lifts up a bowl of olive oil and asks another person to lift up the other bowl of olive oil.)

Leader: People of God, we have been pressed and prodded like olives into oil.

All: Like olives pressed and prodded into oil, we have become new.

Leader: Friends, we are being made into a new creation.

All: **A new creation for God's kingdom here on earth, as it is in heaven.**

Leader: Fellow believers, our study has pressed us so that we might know God's presence more fully.

All: **Our shared learning and insights have pressed us in such a way that we seek to serve God more effectively in this age.**

Leader: We are a community of God's people gathered to be reminded, by this oil, that we are not alone.

All: **That we are affirmed and sent out by the Holy Spirit into communities.**

Leader: The Holy Spirit will hold us. The Holy Spirit defends all that cherishes life.

All: **By the Holy Spirit, we are healed.**

Leader: The Holy Spirit will help us in our struggle against injustices and all that fosters death-dealing acts.

All: **The olive pressed is no longer alone.**

Leader: As a token of this abiding presence of the Holy Spirit in us as our healer, counselor, sustainer, and companion, please dip your finger into the oil and apply the oil to the forehead or the palm of your neighbor, as she or he indicates. While doing so, say to each other,

"The olive pressed into oil is no longer alone. Be courageous, and do God's ministry."

[All continue to sing stanzas 2-3 of "Sois la Semilla" ("You Are the Seed").]

APPENDIX 1

Chapter 1:
The God of the Sharecropper's Farm

Answers:
(1) Yes. (2) Yes. Most probably. (3) No. Acknowledge differences, celebrate differences, while trying to live harmoniously. (4) Yes. The prevenient grace of God operates still. (5) Yes. (6) Yes. (7) Yes. (8) Yes. (9) Spirituality and Social Action should not be separated.

APPENDIX 2
20th Century–Decades of Christian Mission Chart by Robert J. Harman

Decade	1910-1920	1920-1930
Theme	Evangelization of the world in this generation.	Save the world for Christ.
Text	Go ... and make disciples of all nations. Mt. 28:19-20	For God so loved the world .... Jn. 3:16
Events	Edinburgh International Missionary Conference 1910.	Formation of International Missionary Council. Jerusalem Conference 1928.
Emphasis	Proclaim the gospel. Missionary mobilization.	Combat poverty, ignorance. Cooperation. Indigenous churches.

1930-1940	1940-1950	1950-1960
Meeting the world's needs.	Reconstruction.	Christian presence.
God was in Christ reconciling the world. 2 Cor. 5:19	May they all be one... Jn. 17:11	I was hungry and you gave me food.... Mt. 25:31-46
Proposals for forming World Council of Churches. Service units emerging in mission boards.	First Assembly of World Council of Churches – Amsterdam 1948. Formation of International Organizations – UN, World Bank. UMCOR.	Strassbourg Missionary Conference. International Missionary Conference meets in Ghana 1958. Second Assembly of WCC – Evanston 1954.
Integrate evangelism and service. Reconciliation.	Hope in unity. World Council of Churches.	Technical assistance and development.

Decade	1960-1970	1970-1980
Theme	Mission unto six continents.	Confessing Christ today.
Text	The company of those who believed were of one party and they had everything in common. Acts 2:44	The Spirit of the Lord is upon me because he has sent me to proclaim release..freedom…acceptable year of the Lord's favor. Lk. 4:18-20
Events	Third Assembly of WCC in New Delhi 1962. Vatican Council. Human / Civil Rights movements. WCC Delta Ministry in US. Growing influence of Eastern Orthodox thought.	WCC Mission Conference in Bangkok 1972. Call for a "Missionary Moratorium." Base communities with contextual biblical study and theological reflection.
Emphasis	Mission with / by whole people of God.	Solidarity. Human Rights. Social Justice.

1980-1990	1990-2000	2000-2007
Struggle and solidarity and resistance.	Re-visioning and retelling the story.	Transforming church and world.
We are afflicted in every way, but not crushed…persecuted… struck down,… but not destroyed. 2 Cor. 4:8-10	Lo, I am with you always, even to the close of the age. Mt. 20:16	Look, I have set before you an open door, which no one is able to shut. Rev. 3:8
WCC Assembly in Vancouver 1983. WCC Conference on Justice, Peace and Integrity of Creation 1988 Seoul. Anti-apartheid movement. Resistance to US Central American policies.	WCC Assemblies 1990 Canberra 1999 Zimbabwe. End of "Cold War." New role for non-governmental organizations.	Post communist church renewal in Eastern Europe. WCC Assembly Brazil 2006. Emergence of new forms of ecumenical collaboration (Evangelicals, Catholics, Pentecostals).
Enablement and partnership. Misseo Dei Mission and Evangelism.	Poverty and affluence. Shift of Christian axis to the South.	Spirituality encountering globalization.

Endnotes

Session 1

1. The notion of the church being round is taken from my mentor in theology, the late Letty M. Russell, in her book, *The Church in the Round* (Louisville, Kentucky: Westminster/John Knox Press, 1993).

2. Eugene Peterson refers to the phrase "child-of-God's self" in *The Message,* John 1.

3. St. Bernard of Clairvaux in De consideratione libri quinque ad Eugenium tertium, II.1, 2: Migne, P.L. CLXXXII, 745D. Quoted in Henri Nouwen's "Foreword" to *We Drink from Our Own Wells: The Spiritual Journey of a People* by Gustavo Gutiérrez (Maryknoll, New York: Orbis Books, 1997), 5.

4. *The Gospel Train's A-Coming: Beatitude, Suffering, and Ethnicity.* Mission Evangelism Series, Number 2. Editor. Josiah Young III. (New York: General Board of Global Ministries, The United Methodist Church, 1998), 7.

5. Jim Wallis in his *God's Politics: Why the Right Gets It Wrong and the Left Doesn't Get It* (New York: HarperCollins Publishers, Inc. 2005), 29.

6. "Christian Existence in a World of Limits" by John Cobb, Jr. in *Simpler Living, Compassionate Life: A Christian Perspective*, ed. Michael Schut (Denver, Colorado: Living the Good News. 8th printing, 2001), 123.

Session 2

1. *The Prayers and Meditations of Saint Anselm with Proslogian.* Trans. Benedicta Ward. (Middlesex, England: Penguin Books, 1975), 244.

2. Norbert Mette in "Diakonia: Internationale Zeitschrift fur die Praxis der Kirche" quoted in David J. Bosch's *Believing in the Future: Toward a Missiology of Western Culture* (Valley Forge, Pennsylvania: Trinity Press International, 1995), 36.

3. Ibid.

4. A. P. Schmid's distinction between "terrorism from above" and "terrorism from below" quoted in Joseph S. Truman's book, *Communicating Terror: The Rhetorical Dimensions of Terrorism* (London and New Delhi: SAGE Publications, 2003), 14-15.

5. Rufinus of Aquileia, quoted in *Documents of the Christian Church.* Second Edition. Selected and Edited by Henry Bettenson (New York: Oxford University Press, 1963), 34.

6. Taken from *Documents of the Christian Church,* ed. Henry Bettenson, 138.

7. Elie Wiesel in *From the Kingdom of Memory: Reminiscences* (New York: Schocken Books, 1990), 232, 250.

8. Taken from Naim Ateek's sermon, "Christ's Way: The Cross" from *Church & Society Magazine*. Israel and Palestine: The Quest for Peace. (Louisville, Kentucky: Presbyterian Church U.S.A. September/October 2003. Vol. 94, Number 1), 120.

9. Words by Albert Goodson.

Session 3

1. Leonard Sweet in *Post-Modern Pilgrims: First Century Passion for the 21ˢᵗ Century*. (Broadman & Holman Publishers, Nashville, Tennessee, 2000), 28.

2. Leonard Sweet in *Quantum Spirituality: A Postmodern Apologetic,* (Dayton, Ohio: SpiritVenture Ministries, Inc., 2000), 10.

3. *20ᵗʰ Century—Decades of Mission* Chart by Robert J. Harman, retired planning officer of the General Board of Global Ministries and then chief executive officer for the denomination's world mission program, Appendix 2 in this book.

4. Raymond Fung in *The Isaiah Vision: An Ecumenical Strategy for Congregational Evangelism,* (Geneva: WCC Publication, 1992), 43.

5. Mercy Amba Oduyoe borrows the term "hearthhold" from a sociologist, Felicia I. Ekejuiba, and coins the phrase "hearthhold of God" in *Introducing African Women's Theology* (Sheffield, England: Academic Press, 2001), 78.

6. Kosuke Koyama in "The Tradition and Indigenisation" in *The Asia Journal of Theology*, 7:1, April 1993, 7.

Session 4

1. Emil Brunner, *The Word and the World* (London: The Student Christian Movement Press, 1931), 108.

2. David J. Bosch, *Transforming Mission: Paradigm Shifts in Theology of Mission* (Maryknoll, New York: Orbis Books, 1991), 494.

3. W. J. Milligan in his book, *The New Nomads: Challenges Facing Christians in Western Europe*. The Risk Series. (Geneva: The World Council of Churches, 1984), 55.

4. Jim Wallis in his book, *God's Politics: Why the Right Gets it Wrong and the Left Doesn't Get It* (New York: HarperCollins Publishers, Inc., 2005), 141.

GLOSSARY

A Glossary of Selected Theological Terms

Christology: Reflection on, and teaching and study of Christ. Individual or church's understanding of Jesus as Christ.

Ecclesiology: Reflection on, and teaching and study of the church.

Feminist theologies: While doing theology, Feminist theologians focus on the experiences of women, especially their experiences under church and societal patriarchies, male-dominated systems and perspectives. Like the Liberation theologies, the Feminist theologies are also advocacy theologies. They seek to liberate women from systems of patriarchy in order to achieve women's equality with men. Feminist theologians interpret the biblical texts from the perspectives and experiences of women.

Liberation Theologies: The term, "Theology of Liberation," was first used by Gustavo Gutiérrez, a theologian from Peru in South America. Liberation theologies focus on God as a Liberator and God's "preferential option for the poor." The Liberation theologians analyze the systemic nature and contexts of societal oppressions such as economic, racial, political and other oppressions, and call for advocacy efforts to stand in solidarity with the poor in their struggle for justice, peace, and harmony. Liberation is not only freedom from personal sin, but also being engaged in actions that bring about freedom from systems that oppress peoples.

Theology: Study of God. God-talk.

Womanist Theology: Sharing the common concerns of women, along with the Feminist theologians, the Womanist theologians, in addition, focus on the issue of race and racial oppression. African-American female theologians address the racial oppression of African Americans, in general; and specifically, the oppression of African-American women. Womanist theologians interpret the Bible, therefore, from African-American perspectives and experiences, especially those of African-American women.

BIBLIOGRAPHY

Ateek, Naim. "Christ's Way: The Cross." 120-122. *Church and Society.* Israel and Palestine: The Quest for Peace. Vol. 94:1. Bobbi Wells Hargleroad, ed. Louisville, Kentucky: The Presbyterian Church (U.S.A.), September/October 2003.

Bettenson, Henry, ed. *Documents of the Christian Church.* Second edition. New York: Oxford University Press, 1963.

Bosch, David. *Believing in the Future: Toward a Missiology of Western Culture.* Valley Forge, Pennsylvania: Trinity Press International, 1995.

Bosch, David. *Transforming Mission: Paradigm Shifts in Theology of Mission,* Maryknoll, New York: Orbis Books, 1991.

Brunner, Emil. *The Word and the World.* London: The Student Christian Movement Press, 1931.

Fung, Raymond. *The Isaiah Vision: An Ecumenical Strategy for Congregational Evangelism.* Geneva: WCC Publications, 1992.

Gutiérrez, Gustav. *We Drink from Our Own Wells: The Spiritual Journey of a People.* Maryknoll, New York: Orbis Books, 1997.

Koyama, Kosuke. *"The Tradition and Indigenisation."* 69-87. *The Asia Journal of Theology.* Vol. 6, ed. Paul M. Nagano. Claremont School of Theology, California: Center for Asian Studies, 2003-2004.

Milligan, W. J. *The New Nomads: Challenges Facing Christians in Western Europe.* The Risk Book Series. Geneva: The World Council of Churches, 1984.

Oduyoye, Mercy Amba. *Introducing African Women's Theology.* Sheffield, England: Academic Press, 2001.

Peterson, Eugene. *The Message: The New Testament, Psalms and Proverbs.* Colorado Springs, Colorado: Navpress, 1996.

Russell, Letty M. *The Church in the Round.* Louisville, Kentucky: Westminster/John Knox Press, 1993.

Schut, Michael, ed. *Simpler Living, Compassionate Life: A Christian Perspective.* Denver, Colorado: Living the Good News, 2001.

Sweet, Leonard. *Post-Modern Pilgrims: First Century Passion for the 21st Century World.* Nashville, Tennessee: Broadman & Holman Publishers, 2000.

Sweet, Leonard. *Quantum Spirituality: A Postmodern Apologetic.* Dayton, Ohio: Whaleprints for SpiritVenture Ministries, Inc. 1994.

Tuman, Joseph. *Communicating Terror: the Rhetorical Dimensions of Terrorism.* London and New Delhi: SAGE Publications, 2003.

Wallis, Jim. *God's Politics: Why the Right Gets It Wrong and the Left Doesn't Get It.* New York: HarperCollins Publishers, Inc., 2005.

Ward, Benedicta. Trans. *The Prayers and Meditations of Saint Anselm with Proslogian.* Middlesex, England: Penguin Books, 1975.

Wiesel, Elie. *From the Kingdom of Memory: Reminiscences.* New York: Schocken Books, 1990.

Young, Josiah III, ed. *The Gospel Train's A-Coming: Beatitude, Suffering, & Ethnicity.* New York: The General Board of Global Ministries, The United Methodist Church. 1998.

Minerva G. Carcaño

In 2004, Bishop Minerva Carcaño became the first Hispanic woman to be elected to the episcopacy of The United Methodist Church. A native of Edinburg, Texas, Bishop Carcaño spent her early years aspiring to make a difference in the lives of persons facing poverty and discrimination. She has served congregations in Texas, New Mexico, and California, and in 1986 she became the first Hispanic woman to be appointed a United Methodist district superintendent, serving in that capacity in West Texas and New Mexico and later in Portland, Oregon.

Carcaño also was the director of the Mexican American Program at Perkins School of Theology, Southern Methodist University. Never forgetting her roots and early hopes, her ministry has always involved work with the poor, farm workers, immigrants, and refugees, even as she encourages congregations to work ecumenically and to be active in community organizing.

Carcaño's latest work is *I believe in Jesus*, a spiritual growth study for the United Methodist Women's Schools of Christian Mission.

Glory E. Dharmaraj

Glory Dharmaraj is Director of Spiritual Formation and Mission Theology for the Women's Division of the General Board of Global Ministries of The United Methodist Church. She is also the administrator of the United Methodist Seminar Program on National and International Affairs at the Church Center for the United Nations in New York. She gives oversight to the spiritual growth mission study.

She received her Ph.D. from Loyola University in Chicago, and did special studies at Harvard University. She is currently completing her Doctor of Ministry, a joint program at San Francisco Theological Seminary, California, and Ecumenical Theological Education at the World Council of Churches, Geneva, Switzerland. She is an author and co-author of many books, including *Concepts of Mission*; *Mutuality in Mission*, *Many Faces and One Church*, and the denominational mission study on *India-Pakistan*. She is married to a United Methodist clergy.

Additional Resources:

Creo en Jesús. Minerva G. Carcaño.
Guía de Estudio por Glory E. Dharmaraj.
(I believe in Jesus, Spanish translation.)
M3026-2008-01
$7.00

나는 예수¥ '을 믿습니다, 미네르바 까르까뇨
지침ㅇ—: 글로리 다마라지
(I believe in Jesus, Korean translation.)
M3027-2008-01
$7.00

DVD: Through the Corridors of Mission
M3025-2008-01
$4.99

Available from:
Mission Resource Center
800-305-9857
www.missionresourcecenter.org